How to Work with Wood

A Beginner's Manual for Understanding Wood, Essential Tools, and Basic Techniques

James D. Parker

Copyright © 2024 James D. Parker

Table of Contents

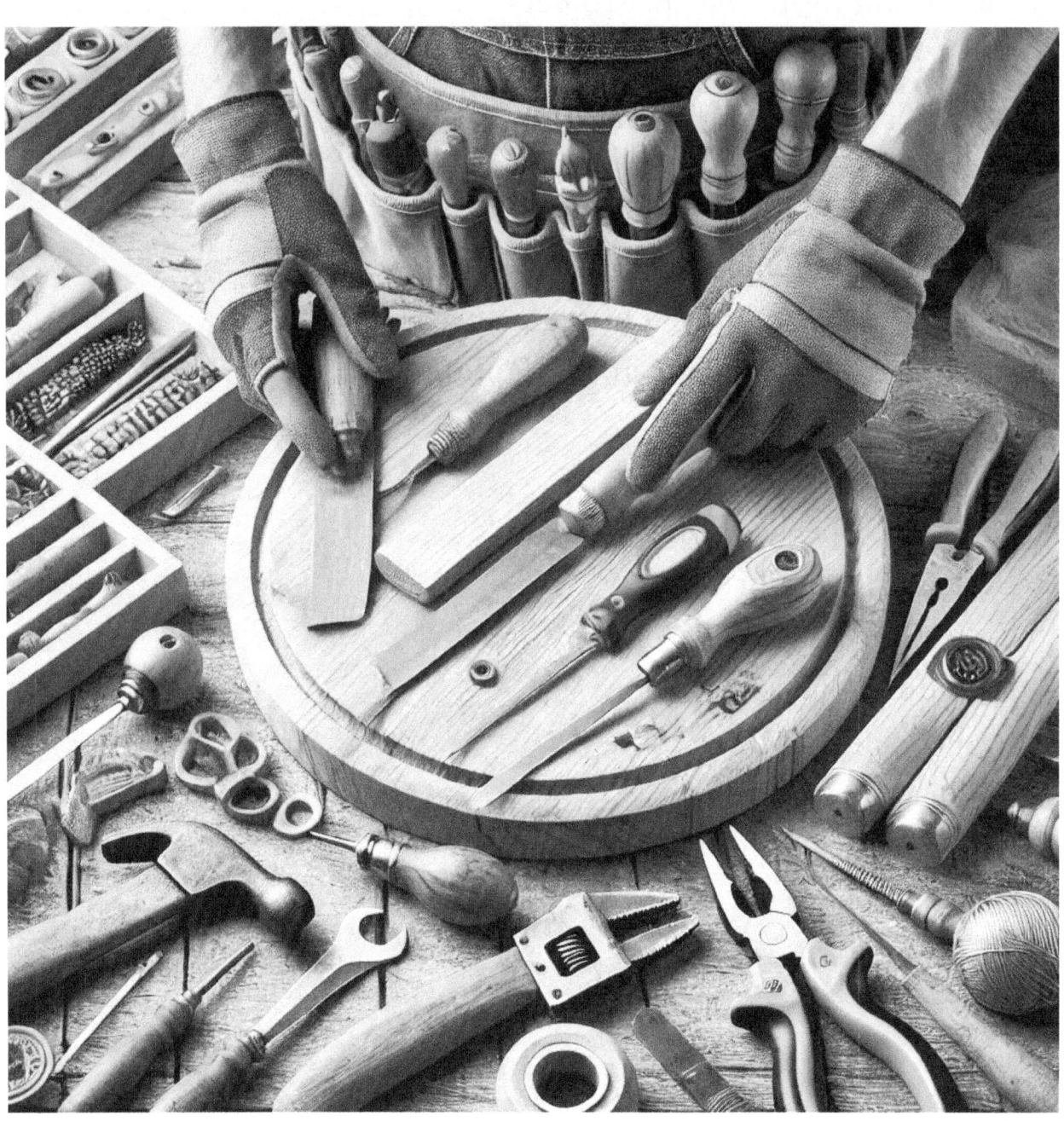

Introduction

Have you ever admired a beautifully crafted piece of wooden furniture and wondered, "Could I create something like that?" Perhaps you've stood in your local hardware store, surrounded by different wood types and tools, feeling overwhelmed by the sheer variety and technical terminology. Or maybe you've attempted a simple woodworking project, only to find yourself frustrated by unexpected grain patterns, imprecise measurements, or unclear project plans. These are common experiences that every aspiring woodworker faces, but they don't have to be barriers to your success in this rewarding craft.

I remember my own journey into woodworking, starting with nothing more than a basic saw and the desire to build something with my own hands. The terminology seemed like a foreign language - quartersawn, bird's eye, mortise and tenon - and every project felt like a leap into the unknown. But through years of experience, learning from both successes and failures, I discovered that woodworking isn't just about following instructions; it's about understanding the fundamental relationship between the craftsperson and their material.

Imagine confidently walking into a lumberyard, immediately recognizing the quality of wood by its grain pattern, knowing exactly which tools you'll need for your project, and understanding how to transform raw boards into beautiful, lasting pieces. Picture yourself reading complex woodworking plans as easily as a favorite book, and envision the satisfaction of creating furniture and accessories that will be cherished for generations. Through "The Complete Guide to Woodworking," you'll develop the knowledge and skills to make this vision your reality.

This comprehensive guide delivers professional insights, time-tested techniques, and clear, practical instruction for mastering the essential elements of woodworking. Whether you're a complete beginner hoping to start your first project or an intermediate woodworker looking to refine your skills, this book will take you from basic understanding to confident craftsmanship. We'll explore everything from the science of wood behavior to the art of finishing, ensuring you have both the technical knowledge and practical skills needed for success.

In this book, we'll journey through:
- The fascinating properties of wood and how they affect your projects
- Essential tools and how to use them effectively and safely
- Fundamental techniques that form the foundation of all woodworking

- Reading grain patterns and selecting the perfect wood for your needs
- Measuring and marking methods that ensure precision
- Understanding and implementing woodworking plans
- Project planning and execution from start to finish
- Problem-solving techniques for common woodworking challenges

By investing in this guide, you're not just acquiring a book – you're gaining access to generations of woodworking wisdom, distilled into practical, applicable knowledge. Instead of learning through costly mistakes or feeling limited by uncertainty, you'll develop the confidence to tackle increasingly complex projects with skill and precision.

Why continue to admire others' woodworking achievements from afar when you can create beautiful pieces yourself? Dive into this guide and discover how to transform raw lumber into stunning crafted works. Are you ready to begin this journey that combines creativity, technical skill, and age-old craftsmanship? Let's embark on this adventure together and unlock the secrets of working with wood, one step at a time.

Chapter 1
Understanding Wood as a Material

The Structure and Properties of Wood

1. Understanding Wood's Basic Structure

Macroscopic Structure
Wood is composed of several distinct layers, each serving a specific purpose:

1. **Bark (Outer and Inner)**
   - *What it is*: The protective outer layer of the tree
   - *How to identify*: Dark, rough exterior texture
   - *Properties*:
     - Outer bark is dead tissue
     - Inner bark (phloem) transports nutrients
     - *Why it matters for woodworking*: Must be removed before processing

2. **Cambium Layer**
   - *What it is*: The growing layer of the tree
   - *How to identify*: Thin, light-colored layer beneath bark

- *Properties*:
- Produces new wood cells
- Responsible for diameter growth
- *Why it matters*: Understanding grain patterns starts here

3. **Sapwood**
  - *What it is*: Active wood tissue that conducts water
  - *How to identify*: Lighter colored outer rings
  - *Properties*:
- Higher moisture content
- More susceptible to decay
- Generally softer than heartwood
  - *Impact on woodworking*:
- Requires different drying techniques
- May need special treatment for preservation

4. **Heartwood**
  - *What it is*: Inner core of mature wood
  - *How to identify*: Darker colored central portion
  - *Properties*:
- More stable
- Natural decay resistance
- Denser than sapwood
  - *Woodworking considerations*:
- Preferred for most projects
- More expensive
- Better dimensional stability

2. Understanding Growth Rings

Reading Growth Rings
- *What they are*: Annual growth patterns
- *How to identify*:
1. Look for alternating light and dark bands
2. Count from outside to inside
3. Observe ring width variations
- *What they tell us*:
 - Age of the tree
 - Growing conditions
 - Wood quality predictions

Types of Growth Patterns
1. **Earlywood (Spring Wood)**
 - Lighter colored
 - Larger cells
 - Less dense
 - Forms during rapid growth period

2. **Latewood (Summer Wood)**
 - Darker colored
 - Smaller, thicker-walled cells
 - More dense
 - Forms during slower growth period

3. Wood Properties Affecting Woodworking

Moisture Content
- *What it is*: Amount of water in wood
- *How to measure*:
1. Use a moisture meter
2. Take readings in multiple spots
3. Average the results
- *Target levels*:
  - Interior projects: 6-8%
  - Exterior projects: 12-15%
- *Impact on working properties*:
  - Affects dimensional stability
  - Influences weight
  - Determines workability

Grain Direction
- *What it is*: Orientation of wood fibers
- *How to identify*:
1. Look for parallel lines on surface
2. Observe end grain pattern
3. Feel surface texture
- *Types*:
  - Straight grain
  - Spiral grain
  - Interlocked grain
  - Irregular grain

- *Working considerations*:
1. Plan cuts with grain direction
2. Adjust tool angles accordingly
3. Consider grain in joint design

Density and Hardness
- *What it is*: Mass per unit volume
- *How to test*:
1. Compare weight of similar sizes
2. Use Janka hardness scale
3. Observe resistance to denting
- *Impact on work*:
 - Tool selection
 - Cutting techniques
 - Joint design
 - Finishing methods

These structural elements and properties work together to create wood's unique characteristics. Understanding them allows woodworkers to:
1. Select appropriate materials
2. Plan projects effectively
3. Anticipate potential problems
4. Choose proper tools and techniques
5. Achieve better results

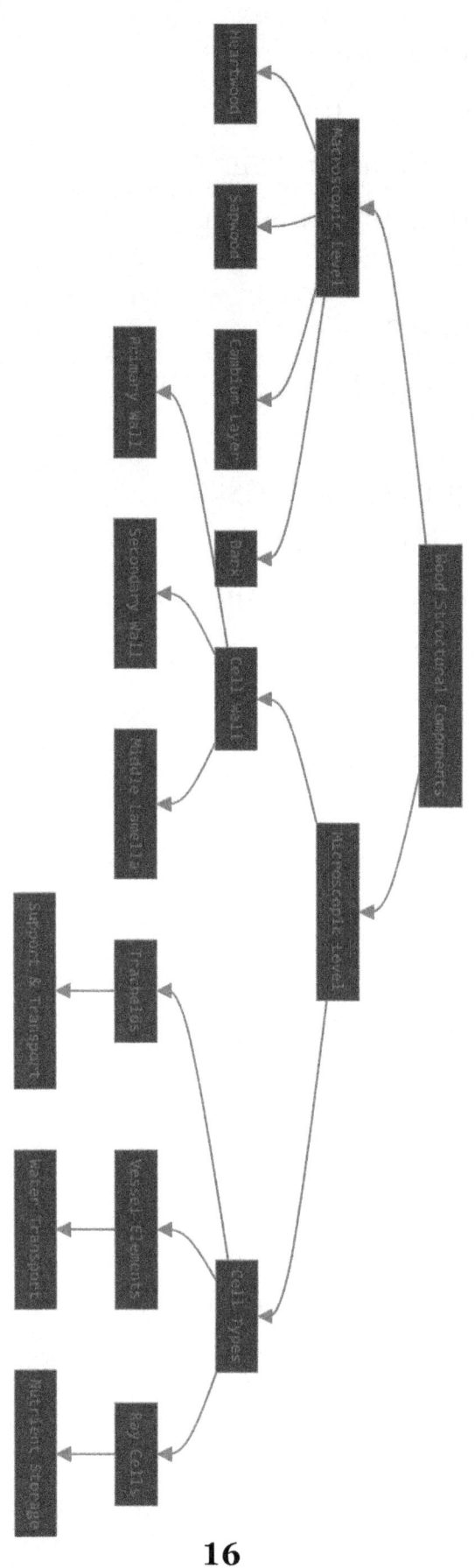

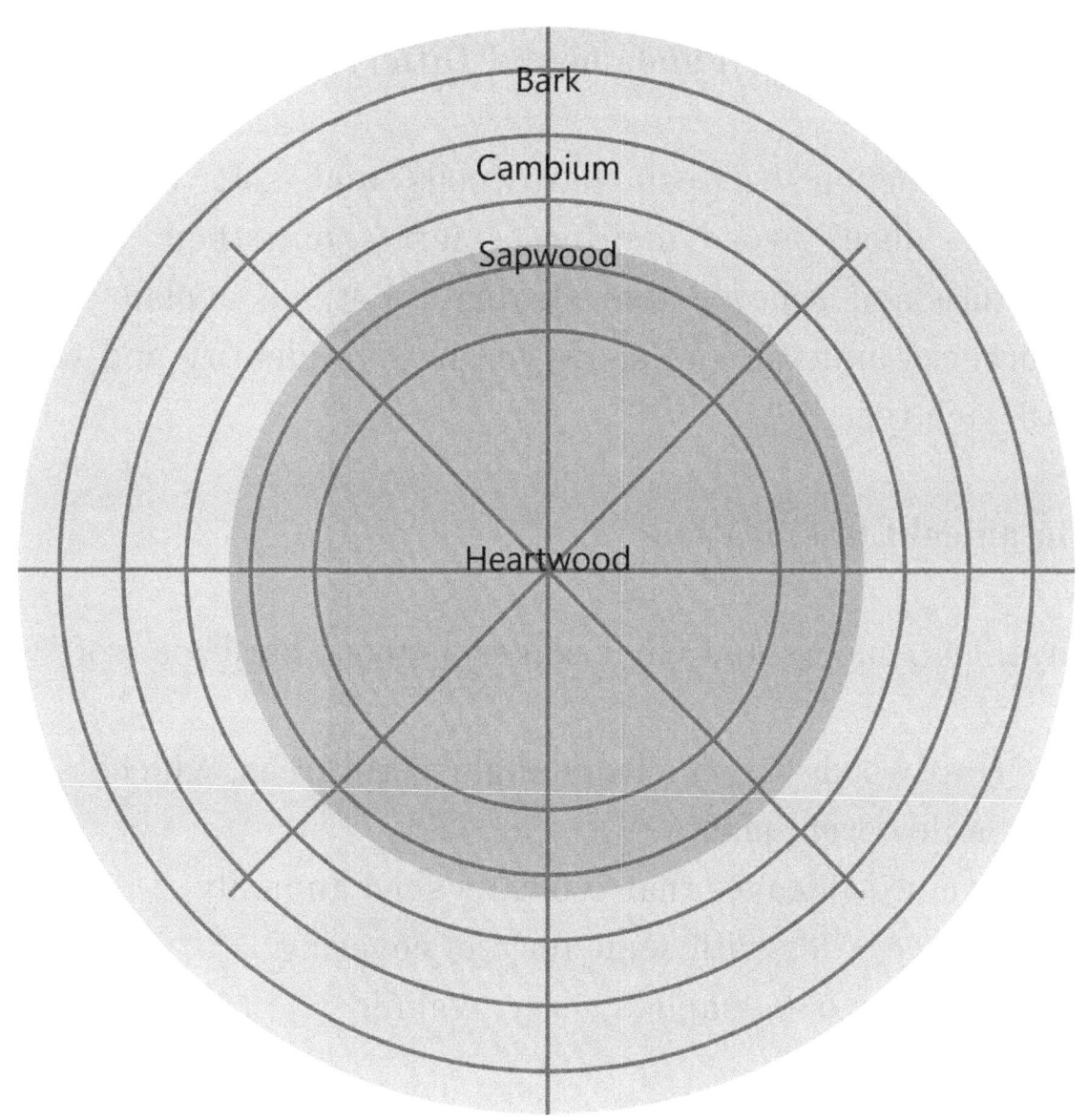

Hardwoods versus Softwoods: A Complete Guide

Understanding the Fundamental Differences

The distinction between hardwoods and softwoods isn't actually about wood hardness—it's about their cellular structure and reproductive strategy. Let me explain these differences in detail and show you how to identify and work with each type.

Botanical Classification

First, let's understand what makes a wood "hard" or "soft":

1. **Hardwoods** come from angiosperm trees, which:
   - Are flowering plants
   - Have broad leaves that typically shed annually
   - Produce seeds with some form of covering
   - Examples: oak, maple, cherry, walnut

2. **Softwoods** come from gymnosperm trees, which:
   - Are typically evergreen (keep their needles year-round)
   - Have seeds that fall directly to the ground
   - Produce cones instead of flowers
   - Examples: pine, cedar, spruce, fir

18

Cellular Structure Differences

Hardwood Structure

Hardwoods have a more complex cellular structure:

1. **Vessels (Pores)**
 - What they are: Tube-like cells for water transport
 - How to identify: Visible as holes in end grain
 - Distribution patterns:
 - Ring-porous (large early-wood pores): Oak, Ash
 - Diffuse-porous (uniform pore size): Maple, Cherry
 - Semi-ring-porous: Black Walnut

2. **Fiber Cells**
 - Provide structural support
 - Create density and strength
 - Impact workability

Softwood Structure

Simpler cellular structure:

1. **Tracheids**
 - Long, hollow cells
 - Handle both water transport and support
 - Create more uniform structure

2. **Resin Canals**
 - Present in some species
 - Can affect finishing
 - May require special handling

Working Properties Comparison

Hardwoods
1. **Cutting and Machining**
 - Generally require sharper tools
 - More likely to tear out due to grain complexity
 - Techniques for success:
 - Use higher cutting speeds
 - Maintain very sharp tools
 - Make multiple shallow passes

2. **Joining**
 - Hold fasteners well
 - Strong glue joints due to cellular structure
 - Best practices:
 - Pre-drill for screws
 - Use appropriate glue pressure
 - Allow longer clamping time

Softwoods
1. **Cutting and Machining**
 - Generally easier to cut
 - More prone to splintering
 - Techniques for success:
 - Use sharp, fine-toothed blades
 - Support workpiece to prevent tear-out
 - Cut slightly oversized for final dimensioning

2. **Joining**
   - May split more easily with fasteners
   - Faster glue absorption
   - Best practices:
   - Always pre-drill
   - Use appropriate screw sizes
   - Watch glue open time

Selection Guide for Projects

When to Choose Hardwoods
1. **Furniture Making**
   - Better wear resistance
   - Superior structural strength
   - More stable over time

2. **High-Traffic Areas**
   - Flooring
   - Countertops
   - Cutting boards

3. **Fine Woodworking**
   - Detailed joinery
   - Carving
   - Musical instruments

When to Choose Softwoods
1. **Construction**
 - Framing
 - Outdoor structures
 - General carpentry

2. **Cost-Effective Projects**
 - Practice pieces
 - Temporary fixtures
 - Large-scale projects

3. **Specific Applications**
 - Cedar for outdoor furniture
 - Pine for rustic furniture
 - Spruce for acoustic guitar tops

Working Techniques

Hardwood Best Practices
1. **Preparation**
 - Acclimate wood properly (minimum 1-2 weeks)
 - Check moisture content
 - Plan grain orientation carefully

2. **Cutting**
 - Use sharp, high-quality blades
 - Take multiple passes for thick stock
 - Consider grain direction for each cut

3. **Finishing**
   - Sand progressively through grits
   - Fill pores if desired
   - Apply finish in optimal conditions

Softwood Best Practices
1. **Preparation**
   - Seal knots and pitch pockets
   - Check for and address resin bleeds
   - Allow proper acclimation time

2. **Cutting**
   - Use zero-clearance inserts
   - Support workpiece edges
   - Choose appropriate blade types

3. **Finishing**
   - Seal before staining
   - Account for uneven absorption
   - Consider grain-filling techniques

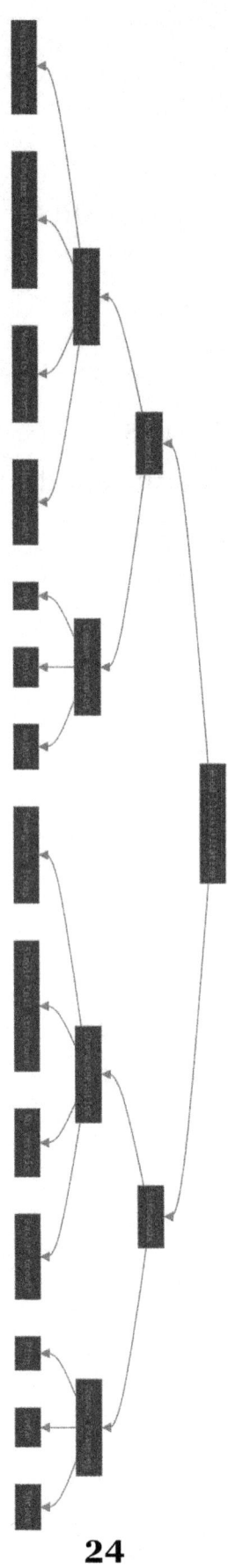

24

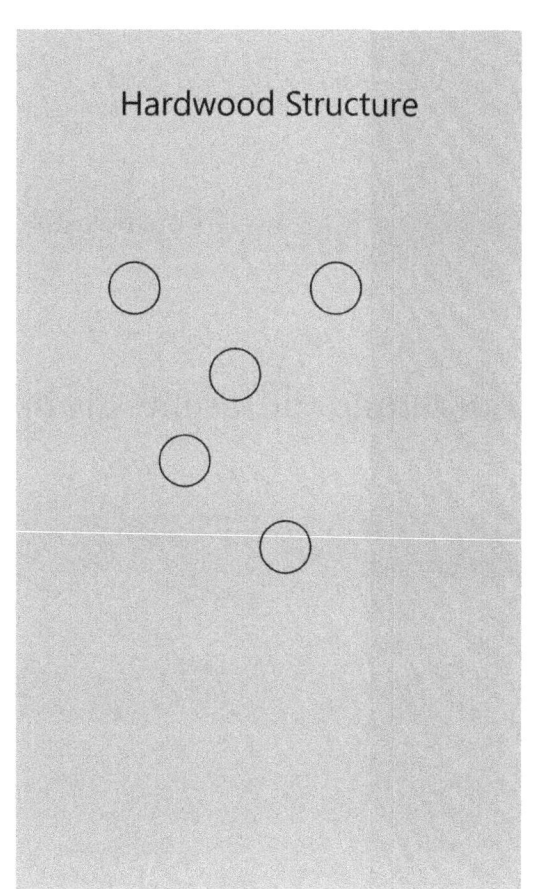

Hardwood Structure

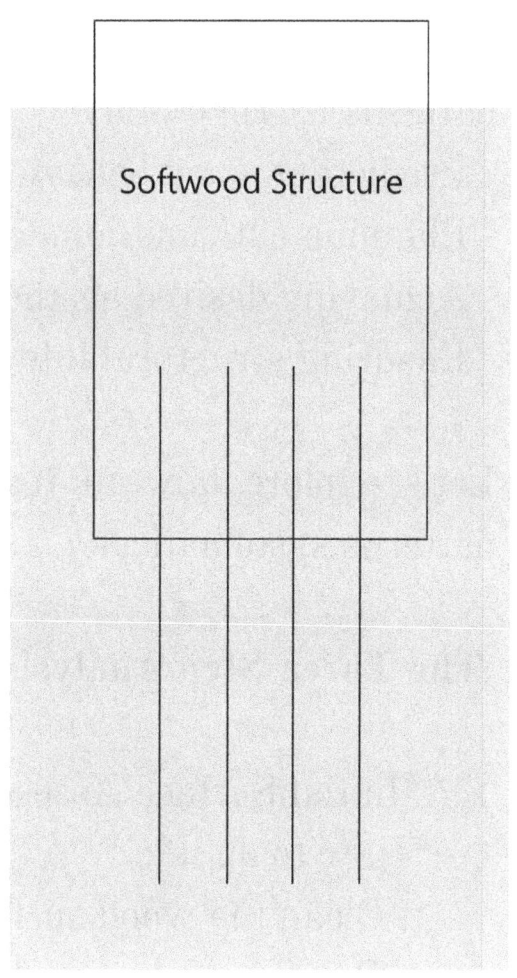

Softwood Structure

Reading and Understanding Wood Grain Patterns

Understanding Wood Grain: The Fundamentals

Wood grain is the direction and pattern of wood fibers relative to the tree's axis of growth. Understanding grain patterns is crucial for:
- Predicting wood behavior
- Planning cuts and joinery
- Achieving desired aesthetic results
- Ensuring structural integrity

Let's explore how to read and understand different grain patterns systematically.

The Three-Step Analysis Process

1. **Initial Surface Assessment**
   - *How to do it*:
     1. Clean the wood surface if necessary
     2. Position under good lighting
     3. View from multiple angles
     4. Feel the surface with your hand
   - *What to look for*:
     - Color variations
     - Surface texture
     - Pattern repetition

- Any figure or unusual patterns

2. **End Grain Examination**
 - *How to do it*:
 1. Look at a clean-cut end
 2. Use magnification if available
 3. Identify growth ring patterns
 4. Note pore arrangements
 - *What to observe*:
 - Growth ring spacing
 - Early/latewood transitions
 - Ray patterns
 - Pore distribution

3. **Edge Grain Analysis**
 - *How to do it*:
 1. Examine board edges
 2. Note angle of grain to surface
 3. Look for grain direction changes
 4. Check for consistency
 - *What to identify*:
 - Grain slope
 - Grain deviation
 - Any irregularities

Common Grain Patterns and Their Identification

 1. Straight Grain
Characteristics:
- Parallel to board edges
- Consistent pattern
- Even texture

How to identify:
1. Look for parallel lines on surface
2. Check if grain runs parallel to edges
3. Observe consistent spacing
4. Feel for smooth texture when planed

 2. Spiral Grain
Characteristics:
- Fibers spiral around tree trunk
- Visible angle to board edges
- Can affect stability

How to identify:
1. Look for diagonal patterns
2. Split a sample piece
3. Observe fiber direction
4. Check multiple faces

3. Interlocked Grain

Characteristics:

- Alternating spiral patterns

- Difficult to work

- Can create ribbon figure

How to identify:

1. Look for alternating patterns

2. Check for resistance when planing

3. Observe changing reflectivity

4. Split test reveals irregular pattern

4. Figured Grain

Types and Identification:

Curly Figure

- *How to identify*:

1. Look for recurring waves

2. Observe light reflection

3. Feel for rippled texture

4. Check pattern consistency

Bird's Eye

- *How to identify*:

1. Look for small circular patterns

2. Check density of "eyes"

3. Observe pattern regularity

4. Note size consistency

Quilted
- *How to identify*:
 1. Look for bubble-like patterns
 2. Check depth of figure
 3. Observe pattern size
 4. Note three-dimensional appearance

Practical Applications

 1. Selecting Wood for Projects
Process:
1. Determine required grain characteristics
2. Examine available stock
3. Consider grain orientation needs
4. Match grain patterns for panels

 2. Planning Cuts
Steps:
1. Mark grain direction on boards
2. Plan cuts to maintain strength
3. Consider grain in joint layout
4. Account for movement

 3. Predicting Wood Movement
Method:
1. Identify grain orientation
2. Note growth ring orientation
3. Consider environmental conditions

4. Plan for seasonal changes

Working with Different Grain Patterns

1. Straight Grain
Best practices:
- Cut with grain direction
- Maintain sharp tools
- Use consistent feed rate
- Plan joinery accordingly

2. Irregular Grain
Techniques:
- Reduce cutting angle
- Take lighter cuts
- Use higher cutting speeds
- Consider grain direction changes

3. Figured Wood
Special considerations:
- Use very sharp tools
- Take extremely light cuts
- Consider scraping vs. planing
- Pay attention to tear-out risk

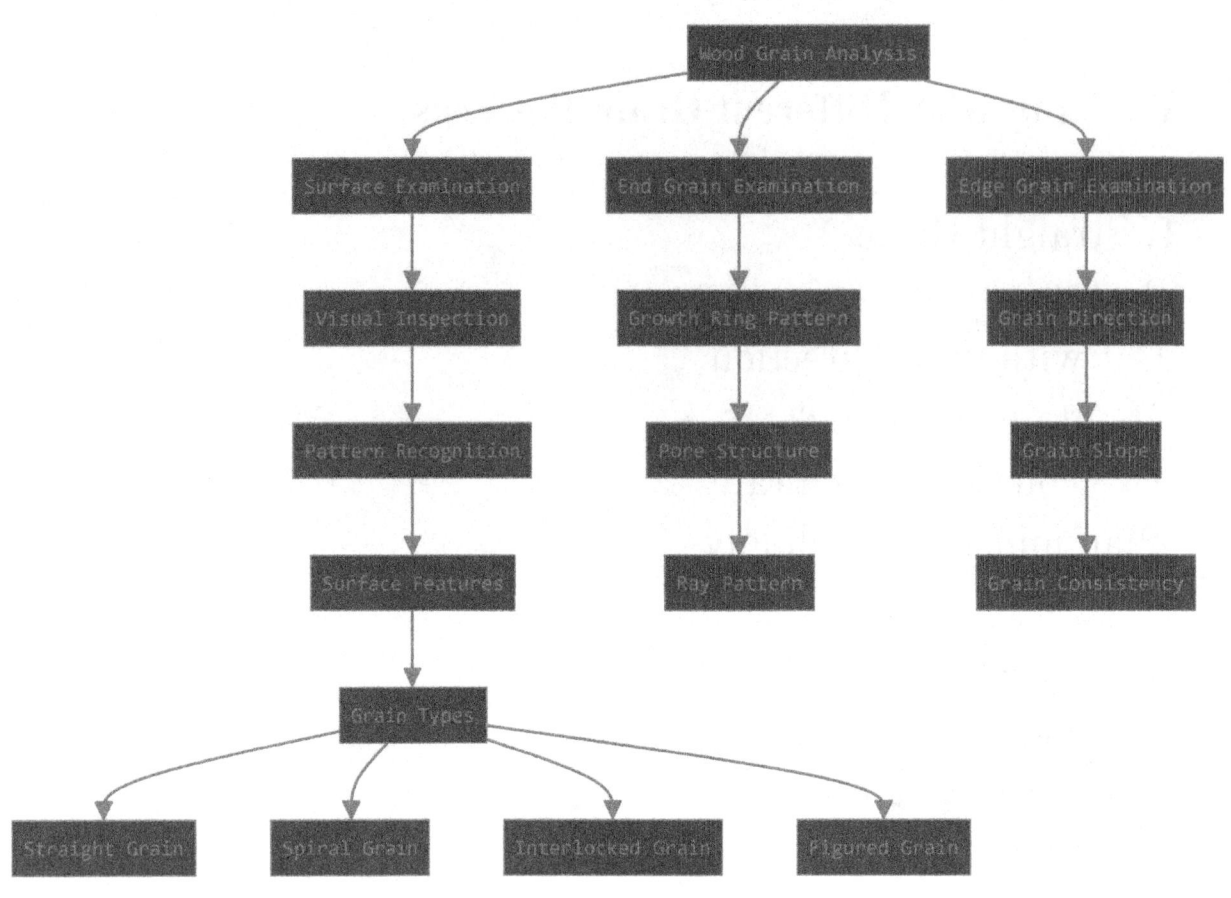

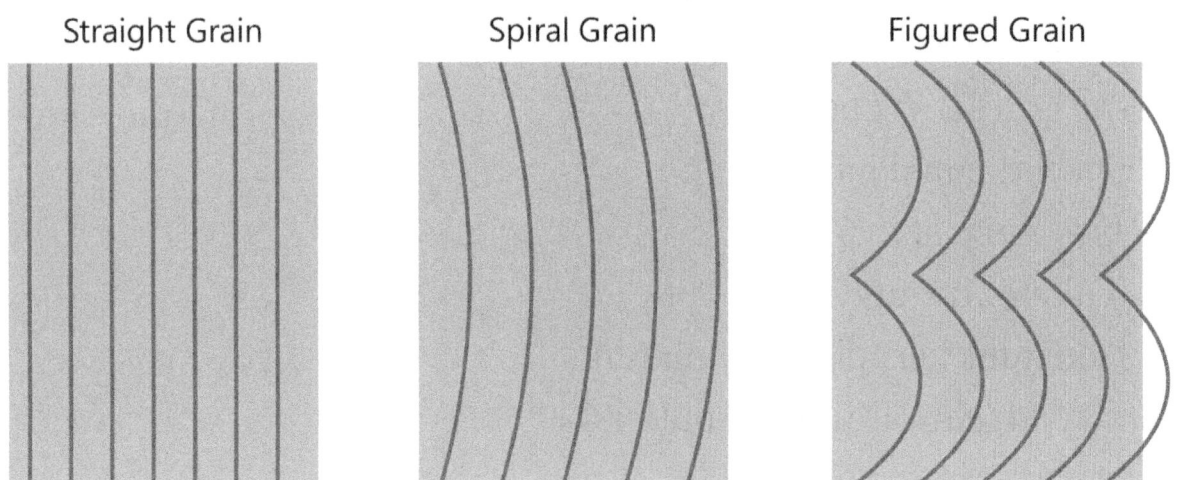

How Weather and Humidity Affect Your Wood

Understanding Wood and Moisture Relationship

Wood is hygroscopic, meaning it naturally absorbs and releases moisture in response to environmental conditions. Let me explain how this process works and what it means for your woodworking projects.

The Science Behind Wood Movement

When we talk about wood movement, we're really discussing three key concepts:

1. **Equilibrium Moisture Content (EMC)**
   - *What it is*: The point where wood neither gains nor loses moisture
   - *How it works*:
     1. Wood adjusts to match ambient conditions
     2. Different environments have different EMC levels
     3. Changes occur continuously
   - *How to measure*:
     1. Use a moisture meter
     2. Take multiple readings
     3. Average the results
     4. Compare to local EMC charts

2. **Fiber Saturation Point**
 - *What it is*: Maximum moisture content in cell walls
 - *Typical values*: 25-30% moisture content
 - *Significance*:
1. Marks beginning of dimensional changes
2. Affects wood stability
3. Influences working properties

3. **Dimensional Change**
 - *Three types of movement*:
1. Tangential (across growth rings)
2. Radial (along rays)
3. Longitudinal (along grain)
 - *How to calculate*:
1. Measure current dimensions
2. Note moisture content
3. Use species-specific movement tables
4. Calculate expected change

Practical Applications and Solutions

1. Measuring and Monitoring

Tools needed:
- Moisture meter
- Hygrometer
- Reference charts
- Documentation system

Process:
1. **Initial Assessment**
 - Take moisture readings of new wood
 - Document ambient conditions
 - Note date and location

2. **Regular Monitoring**
 - Check moisture weekly during acclimation
 - Record changes
 - Watch for movement indicators

3. **Environmental Control**
 - Use dehumidifiers or humidifiers as needed
 - Maintain consistent conditions
 - Monitor seasonal changes

2. Preventive Measures

Wood Selection
1. *Choose appropriate species*:
 - Consider stability characteristics
 - Match wood to environment
 - Account for intended use

2. *Proper storage*:
 - Stack with stickers
 - Maintain air circulation
 - Control environment

Design Considerations
1. *Allow for movement*:
 - Use floating panels
 - Include expansion gaps
 - Design proper joints

2. *Orient grain properly*:
 - Account for movement direction
 - Balance opposing forces
 - Consider seasonal changes

3. Problem Recognition and Solutions

Common Issues and Solutions

1. *Cupping*
 - *Identification*:
 1. Edges raise or lower
 2. Center bows
 3. Surface becomes concave or convex
 - *Solutions*:
 1. Balance moisture exposure
 2. Use proper support
 3. Consider redesign if persistent

2. *Checking*
 - *Identification*:
 1. Surface cracks appear

2. Follow grain pattern

3. May be seasonal

- *Solutions*:

1. Control drying rate

2. Seal end grain

3. Maintain stable environment

3. *Joint Failure*

- *Identification*:

1. Gaps appear

2. Joints loosen

3. Glue lines fail

- *Solutions*:

1. Use proper joinery

2. Allow movement

3. Maintain stable conditions

Environmental Control Strategies

1. Workshop Environment

Controlling conditions:

1. Monitor temperature and humidity

2. Use HVAC systems effectively

3. Implement proper ventilation

4. Consider seasonal adjustments

2. Project Location
Adapting to conditions:
1. Research local climate
2. Plan for seasonal changes
3. Design appropriate solutions
4. Educate clients about movement

3. Long-term Maintenance
Ongoing care:
1. Regular monitoring
2. Preventive measures
3. Quick response to problems
4. Documentation of changes

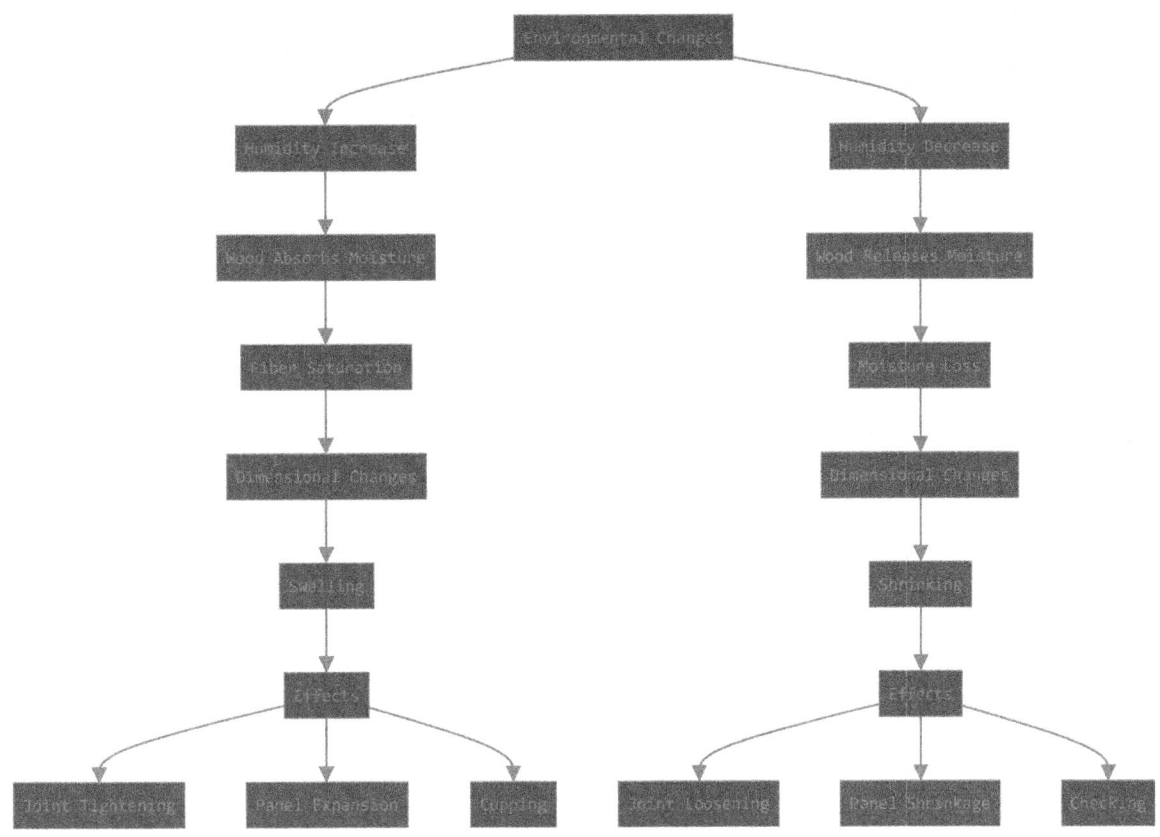

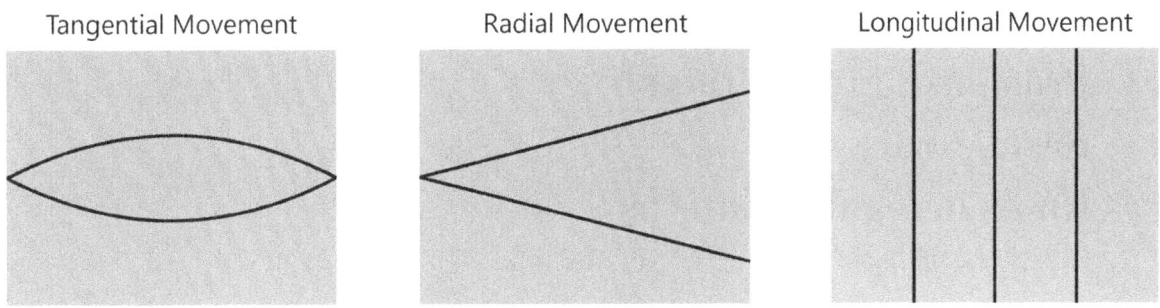

| Tangential Movement | Radial Movement | Longitudinal Movement |

Common Wood Types for Beginners

Understanding Wood Categories

Let's begin by exploring the fundamental categories of wood that beginners should understand. I'll explain each type's characteristics and how to identify and work with them.

Softwoods for Beginners

1. Pine (Eastern White Pine)
Characteristics:
- Color: Light yellowish with brown knots
- Grain: Straight with visible growth rings
- Hardness: 380 Janka

How to identify:
1. Look for:
    - Prominent growth rings
    - Resin canals
    - Knots in regular patterns

Best uses:
- Practice projects
- Shelving
- Paint-grade furniture
- Interior trim

Working properties:
1. Cutting:
 - Use sharp blades
 - Support to prevent tear-out
 - Medium feed rate

2. Joinery:
 - Pre-drill for screws
 - Use appropriate glue pressure
 - Account for softness

 2. Cedar (Western Red Cedar)
Characteristics:
- Color: Reddish-brown
- Grain: Straight, even
- Natural resistance to decay

How to identify:
1. Look for:
 - Distinctive aroma
 - Consistent color
 - Smooth texture

Best uses:
- Outdoor projects
- Closet lining
- Decorative pieces

Working properties:
1. Cutting:
 - Sharp tools essential
 - Dust collection important
 - Light passes recommended

Hardwoods for Beginners

 1. Red Oak
Characteristics:
- Color: Light brown with reddish tint
- Grain: Prominent, open
- Hardness: 1290 Janka

How to identify:
1. Look for:
 - Open pore structure
 - Prominent ray flecks
 - Strong grain pattern

Best uses:
- Furniture
- Flooring
- Cabinet making

Working properties:
1. Cutting:
 - Power tools preferred

- Sharp blades essential
- Steady feed rate

2. Finishing:
 - Grain filling needed
 - Takes stain well
 - Multiple coating required

 2. Maple (Hard Maple)
Characteristics:
- Color: Light cream to white
- Grain: Close, tight
- Hardness: 1450 Janka

How to identify:
1. Look for:
 - Uniform texture
 - Minimal grain pattern
 - Light color

Best uses:
- Cutting boards
- Furniture
- Turning projects

Working properties:
1. Machining:
 - Sharp tools required

- Higher power needed
- Clean cuts essential

Working Techniques for Different Woods

1. Preparation Steps
Process:
1. **Acclimation**
 - Store in workspace
 - Monitor moisture content
 - Allow sufficient time

2. **Initial Assessment**
 - Check for defects
 - Note grain direction
 - Identify problem areas

3. **Planning Cuts**
 - Mark reference faces
 - Plan grain orientation
 - Account for defects

2. Tool Selection and Use

For Softwoods:
1. **Hand Tools**
 - Sharp planes set fine
 - Lower angle chisels

- Fine-toothed saws

2. **Power Tools**
   - High-tooth-count blades
   - Moderate speeds
   - Light passes

For Hardwoods:
1. **Hand Tools**
   - Standard angle planes
   - Robust chisels
   - Appropriate saw teeth

2. **Power Tools**
   - Lower tooth count blades
   - Higher speeds
   - Multiple passes

3. Project Selection by Wood Type

Beginner Projects:
1. **Softwood Projects**
   - Simple boxes
   - Shop storage
   - Picture frames

2. **Hardwood Projects**
   - Small boxes

- Cutting boards
- Simple furniture

Cost Considerations and Purchasing

1. Where to Buy
Sources:
1. **Home Centers**
- Limited selection
- Construction grades
- Convenient location

2. **Lumber Yards**
- Better selection
- Higher grades
- Expert advice

3. **Specialty Dealers**
- Premium selection
- Exotic species
- Professional guidance

2. What to Look For

Selection Process:
1. **Visual Inspection**
- Check for defects
- Look at grain patterns

- Assess color consistency

2. **Physical Assessment**
 - Test for straightness
 - Check moisture content
 - Evaluate stability

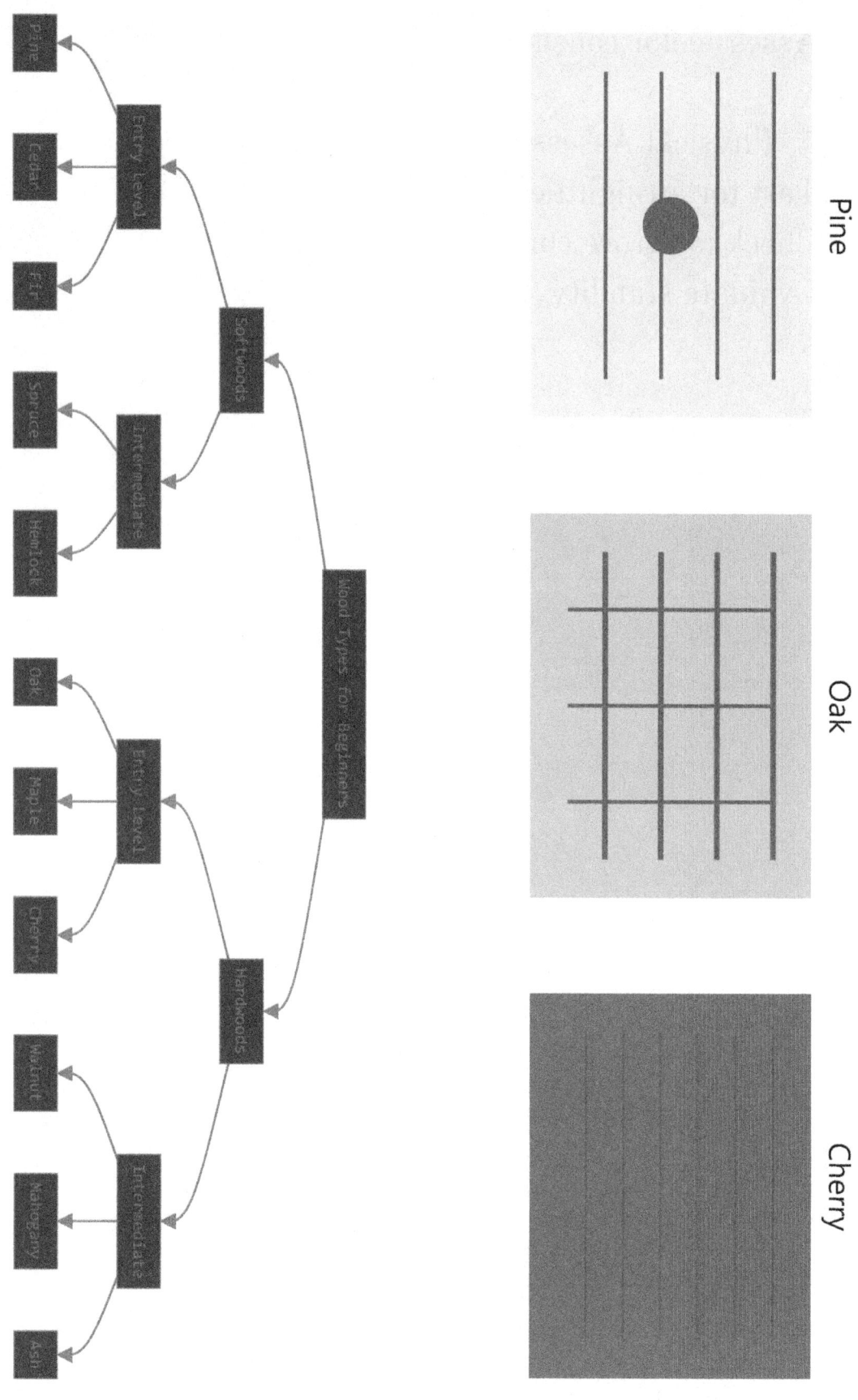

Selecting Quality Wood for Your Projects

Understanding Wood Quality Assessment

Let me walk you through the comprehensive process of selecting quality wood for your projects. This knowledge will help you make informed decisions and avoid costly mistakes.

Phase 1: Initial Assessment

1. Species Identification
Process:
1. Examine color and grain pattern
2. Note weight and density
3. Check end grain structure
4. Consider typical characteristics

How to do it:
- Compare against known samples
- Use wood identification guides
- Consider common local species
- Ask dealer for certification

2. Grade Assessment
Understanding grades:
1. **FAS (First and Seconds)**
   - Highest quality

- Minimum 83% clear face
- Largest clear cuts

2. **Select**
- One clear face
- Some defects allowed
- Good for one-sided projects

3. **Common Grades**
- More defects allowed
- Shorter clear sections
- Lower cost option

Phase 2: Detailed Inspection

1. Moisture Content Evaluation
Tools needed:
- Moisture meter
- Reference charts
- Documentation method

Process:
1. Take multiple readings
- Check both faces
- Test ends separately
- Record measurements

2. Evaluate results
 - Compare to EMC charts
 - Consider intended use
 - Note variations

2. Structural Assessment

Visual inspection:
1. **Check for defects**
 - Knots and their placement
 - Splits and checks
 - Grain irregularities
 - Color consistency

2. **Assess stability**
 - Straightness
 - Twist
 - Cup
 - Bow

Physical inspection:
1. **Surface quality**
 - Run hand along surface
 - Check for roughness
 - Note any irregularities

2. **Soundness test**
 - Tap test for hollow sounds

- Check end grain integrity
- Assess overall density

Phase 3: Project-Specific Considerations

 1. Dimensional Requirements
Process:
1. **Measure carefully**
 - Allow for waste
 - Consider final dimensions
 - Account for machining

2. **Plan cuts**
 - Optimize material use
 - Consider grain matching
 - Allow for defect removal

 2. Aesthetic Considerations
Evaluate:
1. **Color matching**
 - Check for consistency
 - Plan for aging
 - Consider finish effects

2. **Grain patterns**
 - Match for panels
 - Consider figure
 - Plan for visible faces

Phase 4: Cost-Benefit Analysis

1. Price Considerations
Calculate:
1. **Total project cost**
 - Material cost
 - Waste factor
 - Processing needs
 - Finishing requirements

2. **Quality trade-offs**
 - Higher grade vs. more waste
 - Processing time
 - Final appearance

2. Availability
Consider:
1. **Source options**
 - Local suppliers
 - Special orders
 - Alternative species

2. **Lead time**
 - Stock availability
 - Drying requirements
 - Processing time

Phase 5: Making the Final Selection

1. Documentation
Record:
1. **Purchase details**
 - Species and grade
 - Dimensions
 - Moisture content
 - Source

2. **Quality notes**
 - Defect locations
 - Grain characteristics
 - Special considerations

2. Storage Preparation
Plan for:
1. **Transportation**
 - Proper support
 - Protection from elements
 - Secure loading

2. **Storage**
 - Stacking method
 - Environmental control
 - Monitoring schedule

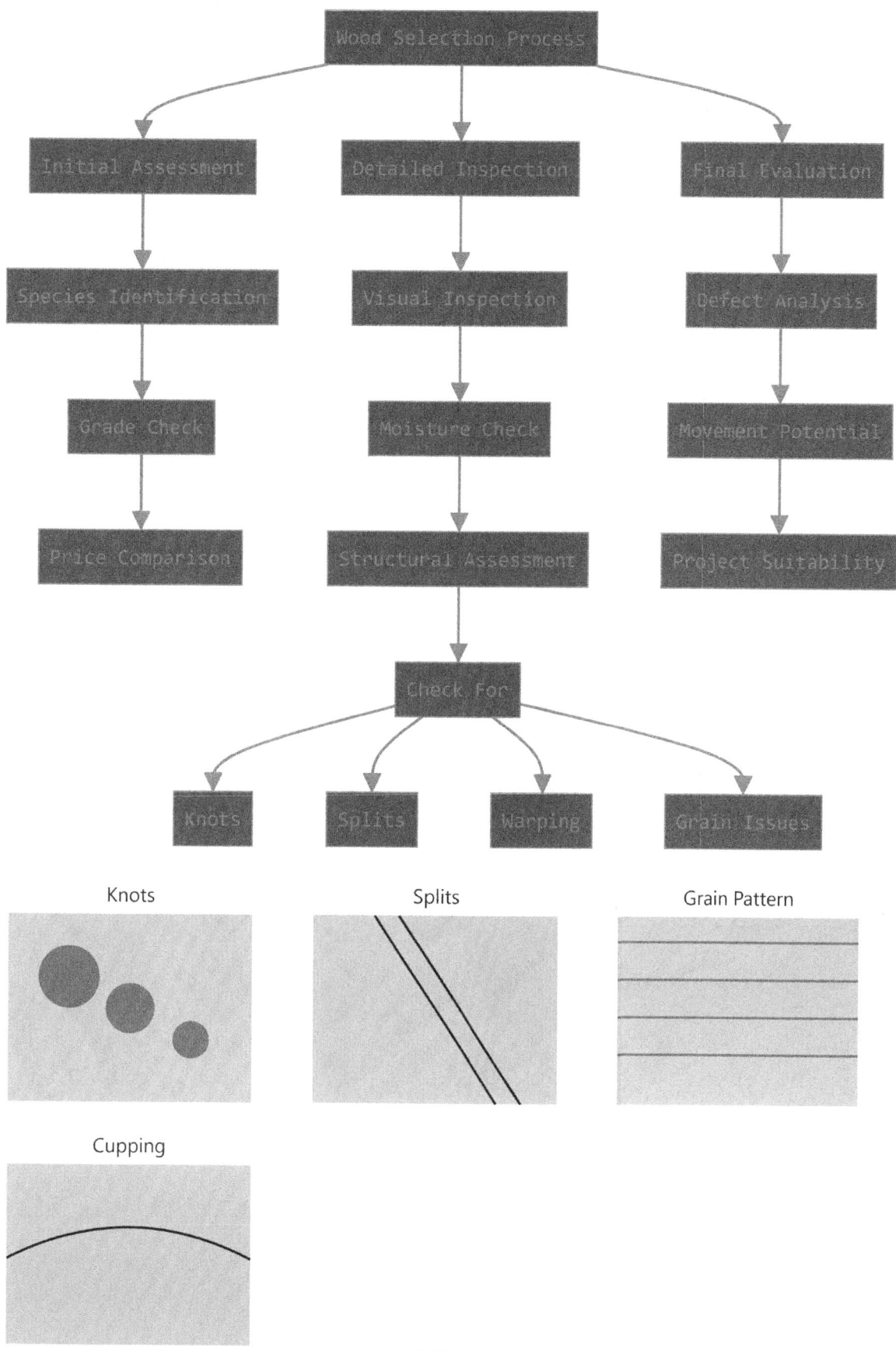

Wood Selection Process

Initial Assessment → Species Identification → Grade Check → Price Comparison

Detailed Inspection → Visual Inspection → Moisture Check → Structural Assessment → Check For → Knots, Splits, Warping, Grain Issues

Final Evaluation → Defect Analysis → Movement Potential → Project Suitability

Knots

Splits

Grain Pattern

Cupping

Chapter 2
Essential Woodworking Tools

Hand Tools Every Woodworker Needs

Measuring and Marking Tools

1. Measuring Tools
Let's start with the fundamental tools for accurate measurement:

 A. Combination Square
Selection criteria:
- Cast metal body
- Accurate 90° and 45° angles
- Smooth sliding action
- Clearly marked measurements

How to use:
1. Check squareness:
    - Place against reference edge
    - Ensure blade sits flat
    - Look for gaps at contact points

2. Mark lines:
    - Lock at desired measurement

- Use as straight edge
- Keep consistent pressure

B. Marking Gauge
Important features:
- Sharp marking point
- Smooth adjustment
- Stable fence
- Clear reference marks

Usage technique:
1. Setting the gauge:
 - Measure desired distance
 - Lock firmly
 - Test on scrap wood

2. Marking process:
 - Keep fence against reference
 - Maintain consistent angle
 - Use light pressure

Cutting Tools

1. Hand Saws
Understanding different saw types and their applications:

A. Crosscut Saw
Selection features:
- 10-12 points per inch
- Rigid blade
- Comfortable handle
- Sharp, well-set teeth

Proper technique:
1. Starting the cut:
 - Score with knife first
 - Start with light backward strokes
 - Guide with thumb

2. Making the cut:
 - Use full blade length
 - Keep consistent angle
 - Let saw do the work
 - Follow marked line

2. Chisels
Essential for fine woodworking:

A. Bench Chisels
Required set:
- 1/4 inch (6mm)
- 1/2 inch (12mm)
- 3/4 inch (19mm)
- 1 inch (25mm)

Usage technique:
1. Paring cuts:
 - Sharp blade essential
 - Shallow angle
 - Control with both hands
 - Work with grain

2. Chopping cuts:
 - Use mallet
 - Keep chisel vertical
 - Take small bites
 - Clear waste frequently

Shaping Tools

1. Hand Planes
The cornerstone of surface preparation:

 A. Jack Plane
Selection criteria:
- Flat sole
- Sharp blade
- Smooth adjustment
- Comfortable grip

Setup process:
1. Blade preparation:
 - Sharpen to fine edge
 - Set proper projection
 - Align square to sole
 - Test cut pattern

2. Usage technique:
 - Start with grain
 - Overlap strokes
 - Maintain consistent pressure
 - Check for flatness

Tool Care and Maintenance

1. Daily Maintenance
Essential practices:
1. Clean after use:
 - Remove dust/debris
 - Wipe with oil cloth
 - Check for damage
 - Store properly

2. Edge tool care:
 - Strop edges
 - Check for nicks
 - Protect from moisture
 - Store safely

2. Regular Maintenance
Schedule:
1. Weekly tasks:
 - Deep clean tools
 - Check adjustments
 - Oil moving parts
 - Inspect handles

2. Monthly tasks:
 - Sharpen all edges
 - Check for rust
 - Verify accuracy

- Lubricate thoroughly

Tool Storage and Organization

1. Storage Solutions
Requirements:
1. Protection:
- Prevent rust
- Avoid damage
- Control moisture
- Secure storage

2. Accessibility:
- Easy reach
- Logical arrangement
- Clear visibility
- Quick return

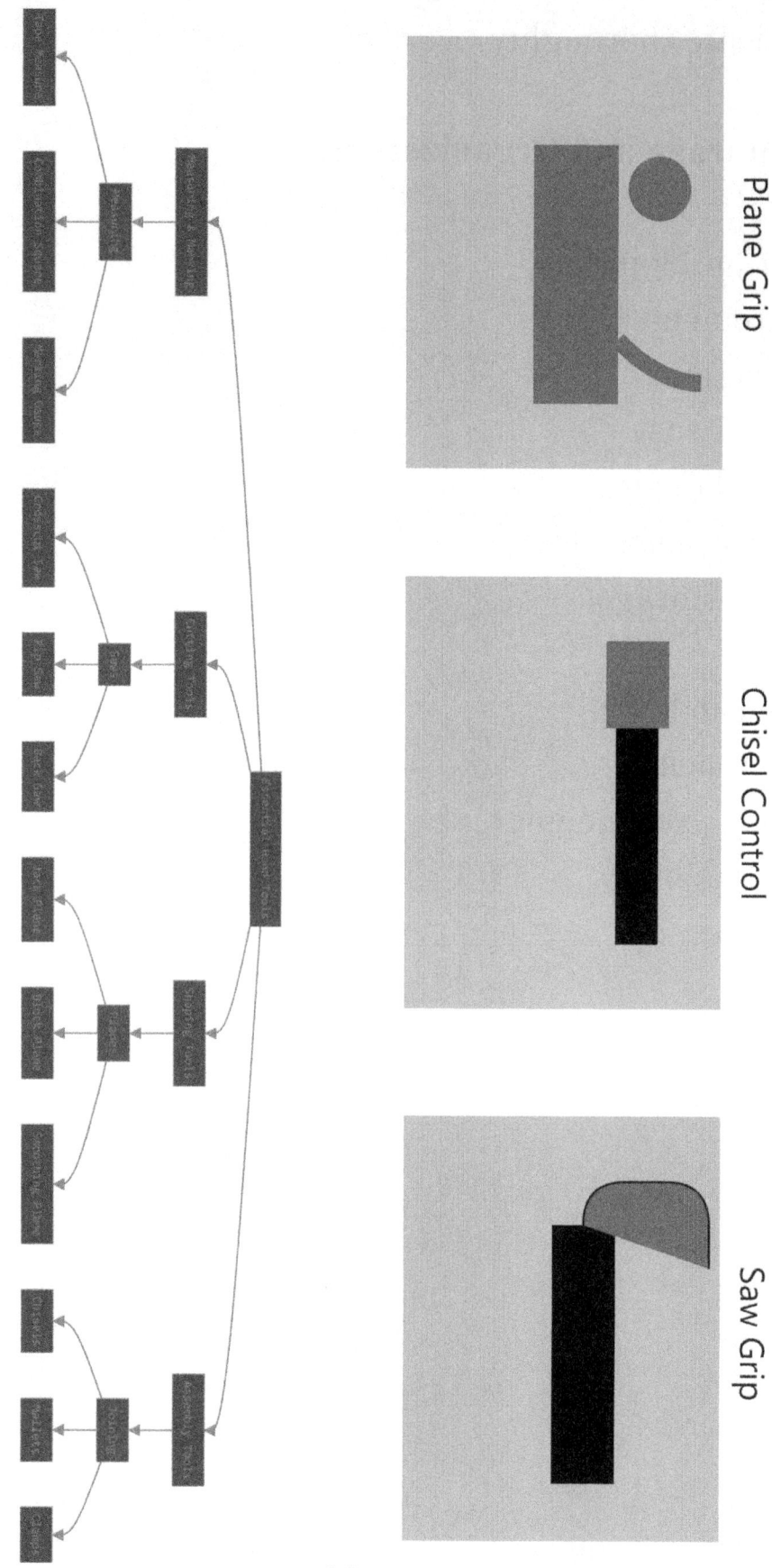

Plane Grip

Chisel Control

Saw Grip

64

Power Tools for Beginners

Let me guide you through the essential power tools that every beginning woodworker should know about, focusing on safety, proper usage, and maintenance. Understanding these tools will help you work efficiently while maintaining safety as your top priority.

The Big Four Power Tools for Beginners

Let's start with the four most essential power tools you'll need, explaining each in detail:

1. Cordless Drill/Driver
The most versatile power tool you'll own.

Selection Criteria:
- Voltage: 18V or 20V for general work
- Battery system: Lithium-ion preferred
- Chuck size: 1/2 inch for versatility
- Brand ecosystem: Consider future tool additions

Basic Operation Process:
1. *Preparation:*
   - Check battery charge
   - Select appropriate bit
   - Set clutch for material
   - Choose speed range

2. *Usage Technique:*
 - Align bit properly
 - Start slowly
 - Maintain straight pressure
 - Monitor heat buildup

2. Circular Saw

Your primary tool for straight cuts in sheet goods and lumber.

Safety Features to Check:
- Blade guard operation
- Electric brake
- Safety switch
- Depth adjustment

Operating Process:
1. *Setup:*
 - Measure and mark cut line
 - Support material properly
 - Set blade depth
 - Check guard operation

2. *Cutting Technique:*
 - Position saw properly
 - Start motor before contact
 - Feed at steady rate
 - Complete cut fully

3. Random Orbital Sander
Essential for surface preparation and finishing.

Key Features:
- Variable speed control
- Dust collection system
- Comfortable grip
- Quick paper change

Usage Steps:
1. *Preparation:*
 - Select appropriate grit
 - Attach dust collection
 - Inspect backing pad
 - Clear work area

2. *Sanding Technique:*
 - Start with power off
 - Light pressure only
 - Keep sander flat
 - Move steadily

4. Router
Versatile tool for edges and joinery.

Important Features:
- Variable speed
- Plunge base option

- Collet size
- Edge guide

Basic Operation:
1. *Setup Process:*
 - Install bit properly
 - Set depth accurately
 - Secure workpiece
 - Test on scrap

Essential Safety Practices

Personal Protective Equipment (PPE)

Required Items:
1. *Eye Protection:*
 - ANSI-rated safety glasses
 - Face shield for heavy work
 - Side protection
 - Anti-fog coating

2. *Hearing Protection:*
 - Earmuffs or plugs
 - Proper noise rating
 - Comfortable fit
 - Regular replacement

Workspace Safety

Setup Requirements:
1. *Power Source:*
 - GFCI protection
 - Proper grounding
 - Cable management
 - Emergency shutoff

2. *Work Area:*
 - Good lighting
 - Clear floor space
 - Dust collection
 - First aid access

Maintenance and Care

Regular Maintenance Schedule

Daily Checks:
1. *Before Use:*
 - Visual inspection
 - Guard operation
 - Cord condition
 - Trigger function

2. *After Use:*
 - Clean thoroughly
 - Check for damage
 - Store properly
 - Document issues

Monthly Maintenance

Detailed Inspection:
1. *Mechanical:*
 - Lubricate parts
 - Check alignments
 - Tighten fasteners
 - Test all functions

2. *Electrical:*
 - Inspect cords
 - Check switches
 - Test batteries
 - Clean contacts

Power Tool Storage

Organization System

Storage Requirements:
1. *Environmental Control:*
 - Temperature stable

- Low humidity
- Dust-free
- Secure location

2. *Access Considerations:*
- Easy retrieval
- Visible storage
- Protected storage
- Logical arrangement

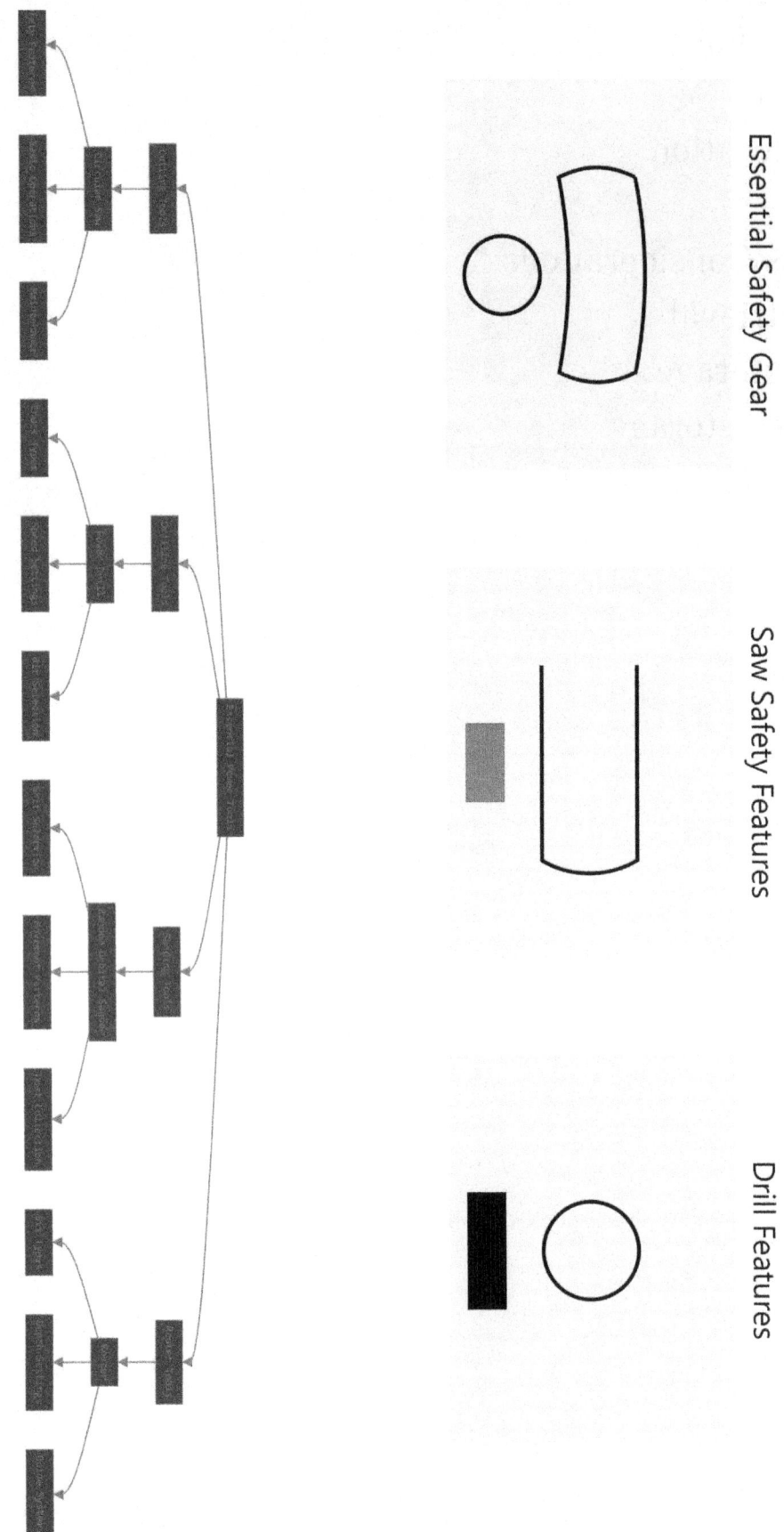

Essential Safety Gear

Saw Safety Features

Drill Features

72

Tool Maintenance and Care

Let me guide you through a comprehensive approach to tool maintenance and care. Proper maintenance not only extends the life of your tools but also ensures they perform at their best and remain safe to use.

Understanding the Maintenance Cycle

Tool maintenance operates on several time scales, each serving a specific purpose in keeping your tools in optimal condition.

Daily Maintenance Routine

The foundation of tool care begins with daily attention. Here's how to implement an effective daily maintenance routine:

1. *Pre-Use Inspection*
   Process:
   - Visual check for damage
   - Verify safety features
   - Test moving parts
   - Check power cords (if applicable)

2. *Post-Use Cleaning*
Steps:
- Remove surface debris
- Wipe down surfaces
- Check cutting edges
- Store properly

Weekly Deep Cleaning Process

A more thorough cleaning process should be performed weekly:

1. *Surface Cleaning*
Materials needed:
- Clean cloths
- Mineral spirits
- Wire brush
- Compressed air

Process:
- Remove all debris
- Clean all surfaces thoroughly
- Inspect for wear
- Address any rust spots

2. *Moving Parts Maintenance*
Steps:
- Disassemble as needed

- Clean mechanisms
- Lubricate appropriately
- Reassemble carefully

Monthly Comprehensive Service

Once a month, perform these detailed maintenance tasks:

1. *Structural Inspection*
Check for:
- Loose fasteners
- Alignment issues
- Wear patterns
- Structural integrity

2. *Calibration Check*
Process:
- Verify measurements
- Check angles
- Test accuracy
- Make adjustments

Specific Tool Care Guidelines

Hand Tools

1. *Cutting Tools*
Edge care process:

- Clean blade thoroughly
- Check for nicks
- Sharpen if needed
- Apply protective oil

2. *Measuring Tools*
Calibration steps:
- Clean measuring surfaces
- Verify accuracy
- Adjust if necessary
- Store properly

Power Tools

1. *Motor Maintenance*
Regular care:
- Clean air vents
- Check brushes
- Listen for unusual sounds
- Monitor performance

2. *Cord and Battery Care*
Process:
- Inspect cords for damage
- Clean battery contacts
- Test charging function
- Store properly

Environmental Control

Creating the right storage environment is crucial:

1. *Temperature Control*
Requirements:
- Stable temperature
- Low humidity
- Good ventilation
- Protection from extremes

2. *Storage Solutions*
Options:
- Tool cabinets
- Wall storage
- Protective cases
- Climate control

Rust Prevention and Treatment

A systematic approach to rust prevention:

1. *Prevention Methods*
Steps:
- Clean tools thoroughly
- Apply rust inhibitor
- Monitor humidity
- Use desiccants

2. *Treatment Process*
When rust appears:
- Identify extent
- Remove surface rust
- Clean thoroughly
- Apply protection

Documentation and Tracking

Maintain records of:

1. *Maintenance Log*
Include:
- Service dates
- Repairs made
- Parts replaced
- Performance notes

2. *Replacement Schedule*
Track:
- Age of tools
- Wear patterns
- Repair history
- Replacement needs

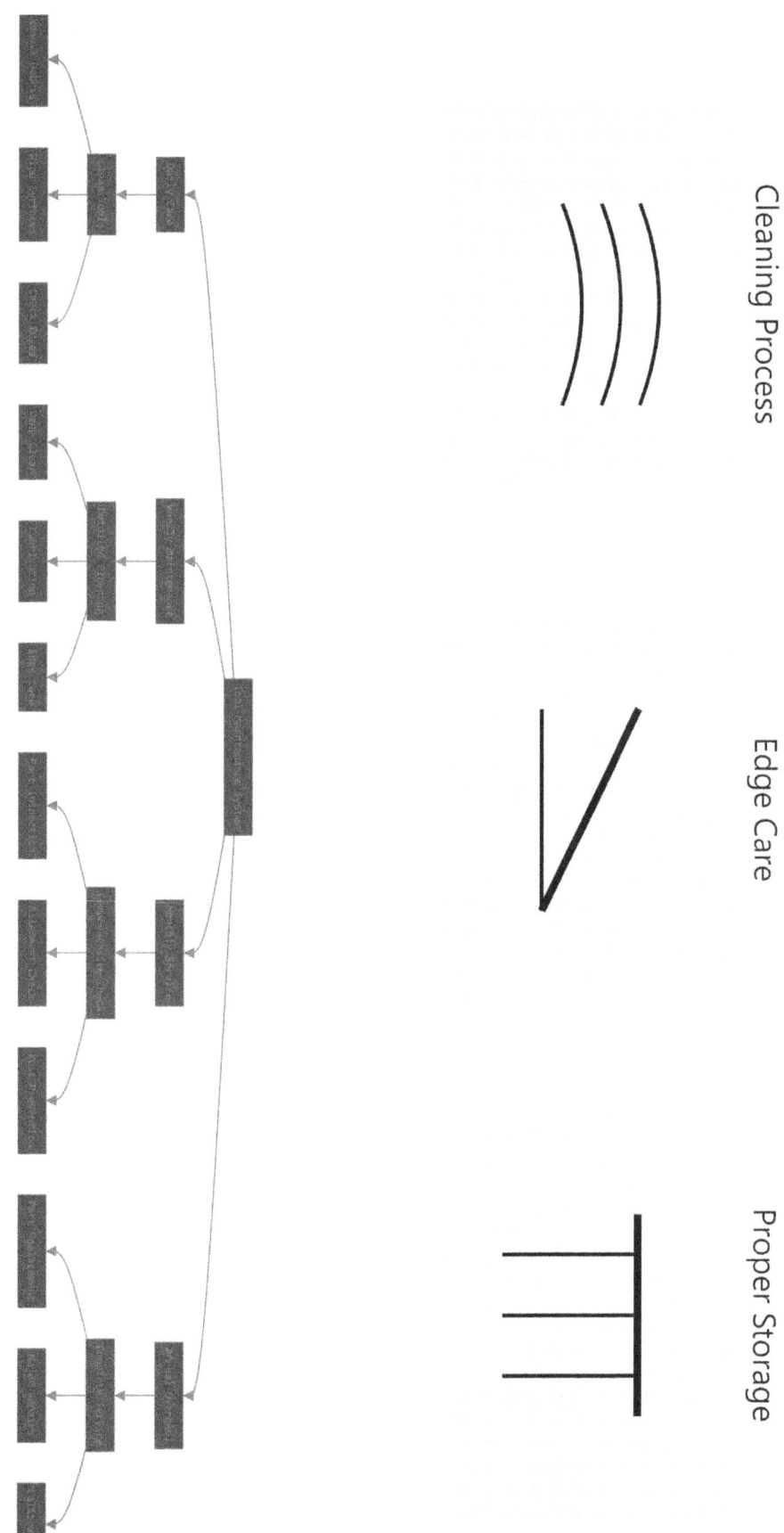

Cleaning Process

Edge Care

Proper Storage

79

Setting Up Your First Tool Kit

Let me guide you through the process of setting up your first woodworking tool kit. This comprehensive approach will help you make informed decisions about tool selection, quality, and organization.

Phase 1: Essential Tools Selection

Let's start by understanding what tools you absolutely need to begin woodworking. I'll break this down into categories and explain the selection process for each.

Measuring and Marking Tools

1. *Tape Measure*
   Selection criteria:
   - 25-foot length minimum
   - 1-inch wide blade
   - Sturdy lock mechanism
   - Clear markings

   How to choose:
   - Check blade standout
   - Verify smooth retraction
   - Test lock mechanism
   - Compare reading clarity

2. *Combination Square*

Selection criteria:
- Cast metal body
- Etched markings
- Smooth sliding action
- True 90-degree angle

Testing process:
- Check squareness
- Verify measurements
- Test blade movement
- Confirm accuracy

Cutting Tools

1. *Hand Saw*
Essential features:
- Comfortable grip
- Sharp teeth
- Appropriate TPI
- Straight blade

Selection process:
- Check tooth geometry
- Test handle comfort
- Verify blade tension
- Examine straightness

2. *Chisels*
Starter set:
- 1/4 inch
- 1/2 inch
- 3/4 inch
- 1 inch

Quality indicators:
- Edge retention
- Handle construction
- Steel quality
- Balance

Phase 2: Quality Considerations

Understanding how to balance quality and budget:

Entry-Level Tools

1. *Where to Save*
Appropriate for:
- Learning basics
- Occasional use
- Simple projects
- Skill development

2. *Where to Invest*
Priority items:
- Measuring tools
- Basic hand tools
- Safety equipment
- Core power tools

Quality Assessment

1. *Material Quality*
Check for:
- Steel type
- Construction method
- Finish quality
- Weight and balance

2. *Brand Research*
Consider:
- Reputation
- Warranty terms
- Service support
- User reviews

Phase 3: Storage and Organization

Creating an efficient workspace:

Basic Tool Storage

1. *Tool Box Requirements*
Features needed:
- Multiple compartments
- Strong construction
- Good accessibility
- Weather protection

Organization method:
- Group similar tools
- Protect edges
- Easy identification
- Quick access

Advanced Storage Solutions

1. *Wall Storage*
Components:
- Pegboard system
- Tool holders
- Shadow board
- Labels

Implementation:
- Plan layout
- Install securely
- Organize logically
- Label clearly

Phase 4: Budget Planning

Strategic approach to tool acquisition:

Initial Investment

1. *Core Tools Budget*
   Allocate for:
   - Essential hand tools
   - Basic power tools
   - Safety equipment
   - Storage solutions

2. *Phased Purchasing*
   Strategy:
   - Start with essentials
   - Add as needed
   - Upgrade gradually
   - Watch for sales

Long-term Investment

1. *Tool Upgrade Path*
   Planning for:
   - Quality improvements
   - Capability expansion
   - Specialization
   - Professional tools

2. *Maintenance Budget*
Include:
- Sharpening supplies
- Replacement parts
- Cleaning materials
- Storage upgrades

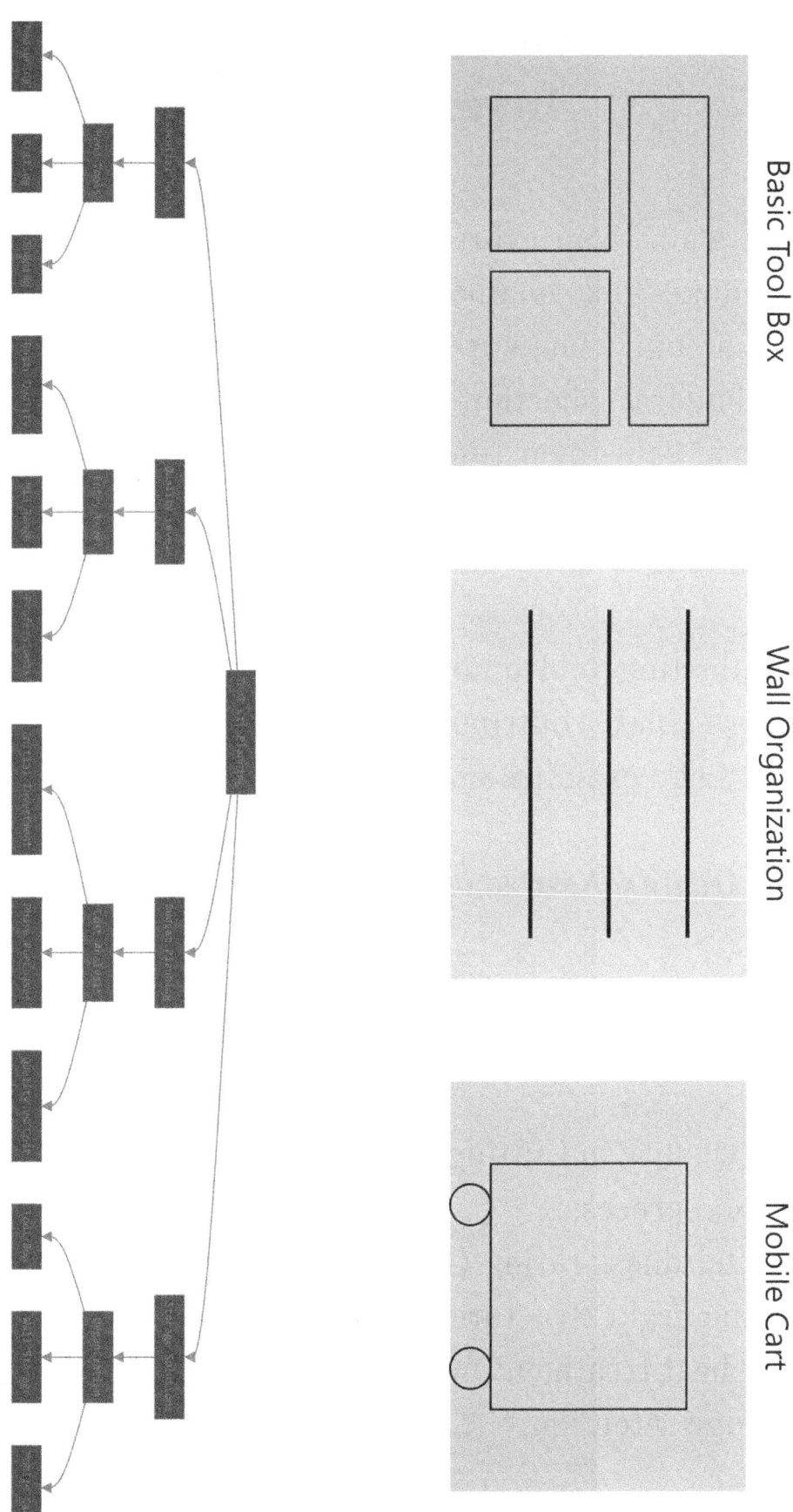

Basic Tool Box

Wall Organization

Mobile Cart

87

Understanding Tool Quality and Investment

Let me walk you through the complex process of understanding tool quality and making wise investment decisions in your woodworking journey. This knowledge will help you build a collection of tools that serve you well and provide good value over time.

Understanding Quality Indicators

When evaluating tool quality, we need to consider several key factors that contribute to overall performance and longevity. Let's examine each in detail:

Material Quality Assessment

The foundation of any tool's quality lies in its materials. Here's how to evaluate them:

1. *Metal Quality in Cutting Tools*
   Evaluation process:
   - Check hardness rating (RC scale)
   - Examine grain structure
   - Verify heat treatment marks
   - Test edge retention

How to test:
- Use a file test for hardness
- Observe spark pattern
- Check magnetic properties
- Evaluate surface finish

2. *Handle Materials*
Quality indicators:
- Grain orientation in wood
- Density and weight
- Surface finish
- Joint construction

Assessment method:
- Check grain alignment
- Test grip comfort
- Evaluate balance
- Inspect finishing quality

Construction Quality Evaluation

The way a tool is put together greatly affects its performance and durability:

1. *Joint and Connection Analysis*
Look for:
- Clean welding lines
- Tight fitting parts

- Proper alignment
- Quality fasteners

Testing process:
- Check for play in joints
- Verify smooth operation
- Test under load
- Examine stress points

2. *Assembly Quality*
Key indicators:
- Component fit
- Moving part smoothness
- Surface transitions
- Overall balance

Investment Strategy Development

Creating a smart investment strategy ensures you get the best value for your money:

Initial Investment Planning

1. *Budget Allocation*
Process:
- Set total budget
- Prioritize essential tools
- Research price ranges

- Plan purchase timing

Implementation:
- Create priority list
- Compare options
- Monitor sales
- Track expenses

2. *Quality Tiers*
Understanding levels:
- Entry-level characteristics
- Mid-range features
- Professional grade attributes
- Specialty tool considerations

Long-term Value Assessment

1. *Cost per Use Calculation*
Formula:
```

Value = (Purchase Price + Maintenance Costs) / Expected
Lifetime Uses
```

Considerations:
- Frequency of use
- Maintenance requirements
- Replacement costs

- Resale value

2. *Lifetime Cost Analysis*
Factors to consider:
- Initial purchase price
- Maintenance expenses
- Upgrade potential
- Replacement timeline

Brand Research and Evaluation

Understanding tool manufacturers helps make informed decisions:

Brand Assessment Criteria

1. *Company History*
Research:
- Years in business
- Manufacturing locations
- Innovation history
- Market reputation

2. *Support Structure*
Evaluate:
- Warranty terms
- Service network
- Parts availability

- Technical support

Quality Control Standards

1. *Manufacturing Standards*
Look for:
- ISO certifications
- Quality control processes
- Testing procedures
- Material standards

2. *Consistency Measures*
Verify:
- Production oversight
- Quality guarantees
- Return policies
- User feedback

Making the Final Decision

Bringing all factors together for informed purchases:

Decision Matrix Creation

1. *Essential Criteria*
Include:
- Quality requirements
- Budget constraints

- Usage needs
- Long-term value

2. *Comparison Process*
Steps:
- Research options
- Compare features
- Read reviews
- Test if possible

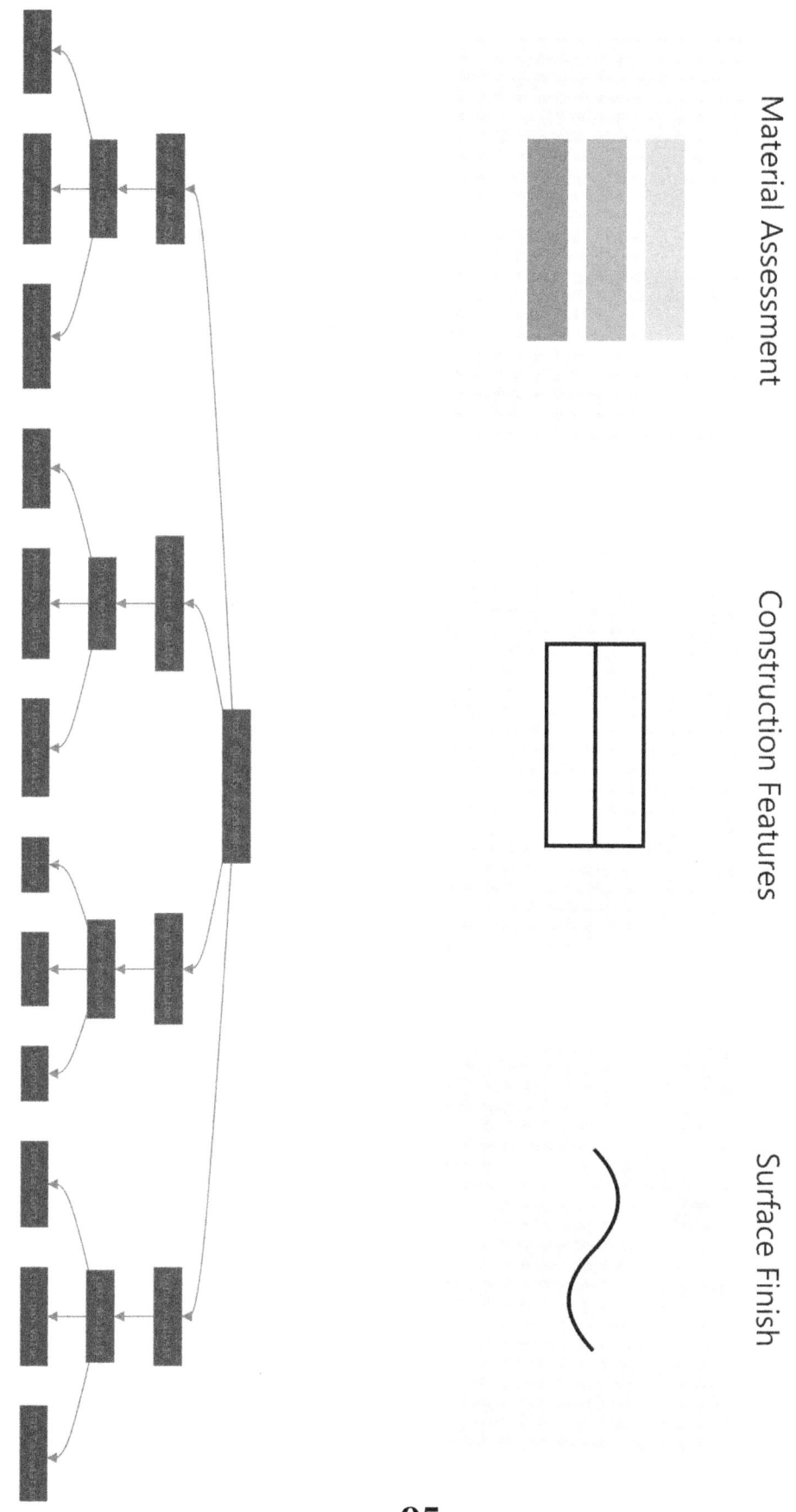

Material Assessment

Construction Features

Surface Finish

Chapter 3
Measuring and Marking Fundamentals

Essential Measuring Tools

When we approach woodworking measurement, accuracy is absolutely crucial. Let me explain how to master the essential measuring tools that form the foundation of precise woodworking. Understanding these tools and their proper use will help prevent costly mistakes and ensure project success.

Linear Measurement Tools

Let's begin with the most fundamental measuring tools and how to use them effectively:

1. Tape Measure Mastery
The tape measure is your most frequently used measuring tool. Here's how to use it properly:

Selection Criteria:
- Choose a tape with clear, readable markings
- Look for a sturdy hook with minimal play
- Ensure smooth extension and retraction
- Verify accuracy against a known standard

Usage Technique:
1. Reading Measurements
 - Account for the hook thickness
 - Keep the tape parallel to the measurement line
 - Read from directly above to avoid parallax error
 - Use the same reference point consistently

2. Common Errors to Avoid
 - Not accounting for hook movement
 - Reading at an angle
 - Failing to maintain tension
 - Inconsistent starting points

2. Rules and Straightedges

Types and Applications:
1. Steel Rule
 - For precise short measurements
 - When reading direct measurements
 - As a straightedge reference
 - For setup and calibration

2. Folding Rule
 - Inside measurements
 - Rough layouts
 - When flexibility isn't needed
 - Long straight measurements

Angular Measurement Tools

Understanding and using tools for measuring and marking angles:

1. Combination Square
A versatile tool that serves multiple functions:

Components and Features:
- Square head for 90° and 45° angles
- Ruled blade for measurements
- Level vial for plumb checks
- Scribe line capability

Usage Steps:
1. Checking Squareness
 - Clean mating surfaces
 - Position square firmly
 - Look for light gaps
 - Mark perpendicular lines

2. Setting Depths and Heights
 - Lock blade at desired measurement
 - Use as depth gauge
 - Transfer measurements
 - Mark parallel lines

2. Try Square

For quick, accurate 90° checks:

Selection Features:
- Solid blade-to-stock joint
- True square alignment
- Clearly marked graduations
- Comfortable handling

Testing Accuracy:
1. Draw a line using the square
2. Flip the square over
3. Compare the line alignment
4. Adjust technique if needed

Layout Tools

Essential tools for transferring measurements:

1. Marking Gauge

For parallel line marking:

Setup Process:
1. Set the distance
  - Measure from fence to pin
  - Lock setting firmly
  - Test on scrap
  - Adjust as needed

2. Making the Mark
 - Keep fence against reference
 - Maintain consistent pressure
 - Score once only
 - Check mark quality

2. Dividers and Calipers
For precise measurement transfer:

Usage Techniques:
1. Setting the Measurement
 - Open to approximate size
 - Fine-tune adjustment
 - Lock setting if applicable
 - Verify setting

2. Transferring Measurements
 - Keep points perpendicular
 - Use consistent pressure
 - Mark clearly
 - Double-check accuracy

Maintenance and Care

Keeping measuring tools accurate:

1. Regular Checks
Verification Process:
1. Compare against standards
2. Check for damage
3. Clean thoroughly
4. Store properly

2. Storage Requirements
Proper Storage:
1. Clean before storing
2. Use protective covers
3. Store in dry location
4. Avoid temperature extremes

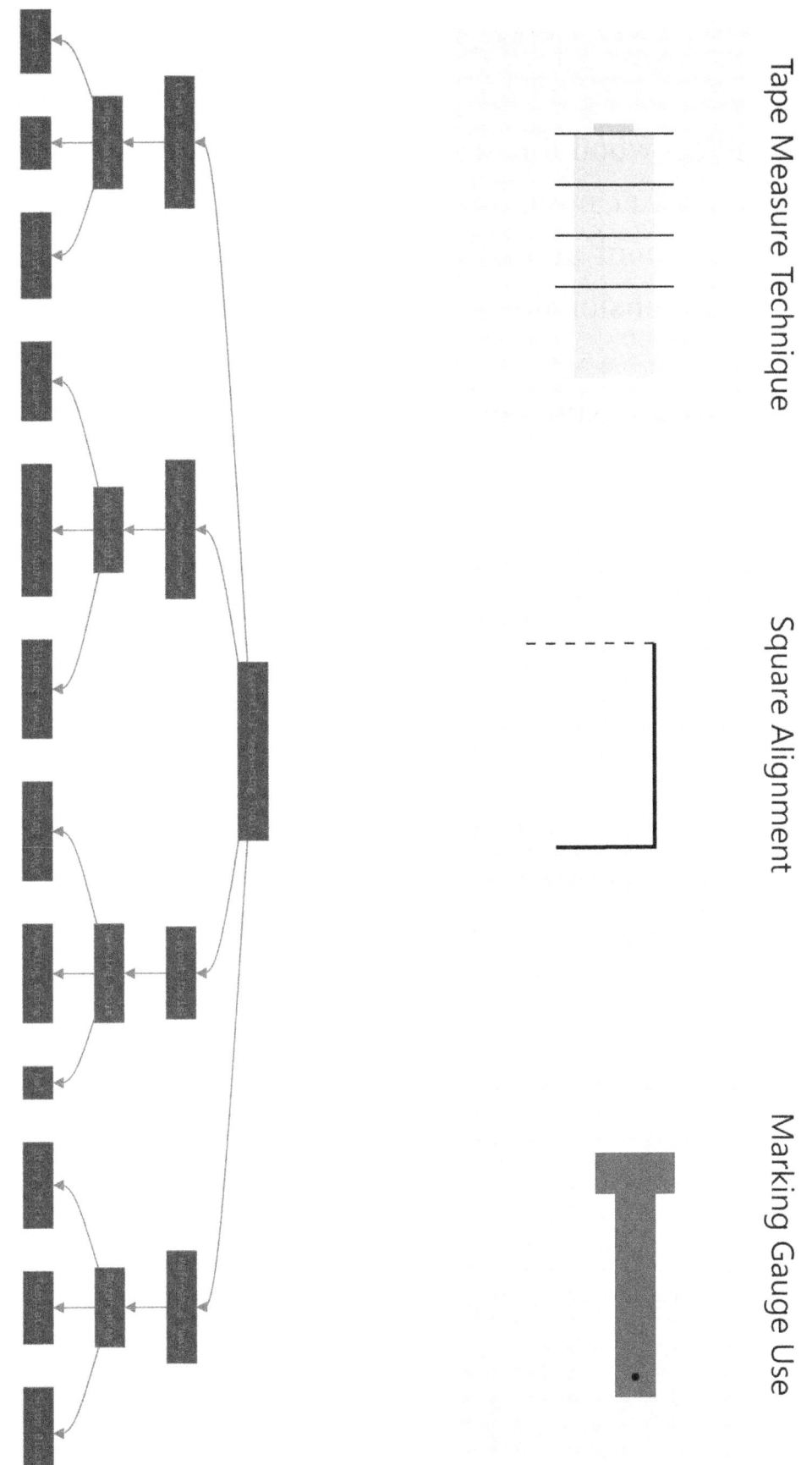

Tape Measure Technique

Square Alignment

Marking Gauge Use

103

Understanding Wood Dimensions

Understanding wood dimensions is fundamental to successful woodworking. Let me guide you through the complexities of wood measurement and help you understand how to account for various dimensional considerations in your projects.

The Three Dimensions of Wood

Wood dimensions can be quite confusing because there are three different ways to measure wood: nominal size, actual size, and working size. Let's explore each of these in detail.

Nominal Dimensions

Nominal dimensions are the traditional names we use when referring to lumber. Here's what you need to know:

1. *Understanding Nominal Sizes*
   The naming system originated from rough-cut lumber dimensions:
   - A "2x4" started as a rough-cut piece measuring 2 inches by 4 inches
   - The milling process reduces these dimensions
   - Final dimensions are standardized

How to interpret:
- Learn common nominal sizes
- Know corresponding actual sizes
- Use reference charts when needed
- Account for regional variations

2. *Common Nominal Sizes*
Standard lumber dimensions:
- 1x material (boards)
- 2x material (dimensional lumber)
- 4x material (posts)
- Sheet goods (plywood, MDF)

Actual Dimensions

Actual dimensions refer to the real measurements of processed lumber:

1. *Standard Reductions*
Understanding the process:
- Rough cutting removes approximately 1/8 inch
- Planing removes another 1/8 inch
- Each face loses about 1/4 inch total

Calculation method:
- Measure all dimensions
- Record actual sizes
- Compare to nominal

- Document variations

2. *Common Actual Sizes*
Examples:
- 2x4 = 1.5" x 3.5"
- 1x6 = 0.75" x 5.5"
- 4x4 = 3.5" x 3.5"
- Sheet goods = 0.75" x 48" x 96"

Working Dimensions

Working dimensions are the final sizes needed for your project:

1. *Determining Working Size*
Process:
- Start with finished dimensions
- Add for joinery
- Include waste allowance
- Consider wood movement

Calculation steps:
1. Identify final size needed
2. Add joinery allowances
3. Include safety margin
4. Document requirements

Measuring Techniques

Proper measurement is crucial for accurate dimensioning:

1. Length Measurement

Process:
1. *Initial Measurement*
 - Use appropriate tool
 - Account for end conditions
 - Mark clearly
 - Double-check

2. *Cutting Allowance*
 - Add for saw kerf
 - Include clean-up cuts
 - Consider grain matching
 - Plan for mistakes

2. Width Measurement

Technique:
1. *Measuring Steps*
 - Check multiple points
 - Account for taper
 - Consider grain orientation
 - Mark reference edge

2. *Width Considerations*
- Allow for seasonal movement
- Account for joinery
- Consider aesthetics
- Plan panel layouts

3. Thickness Measurement

Process:
1. *Gauging Thickness*
- Use calibrated tools
- Check multiple points
- Record variations
- Plan milling sequence

2. *Thickness Planning*
- Account for surfacing
- Allow for sanding
- Consider structural needs
- Plan for final thickness

Dimension Documentation

Keeping track of dimensions:

1. Project Planning
Documentation process:
1. Create cutting diagram

2. List all dimensions

3. Calculate material needs

4. Include waste factor

 2. Material Lists

Organization method:

1. Group similar sizes

2. Note grain requirements

3. Include extra material

4. Document special needs

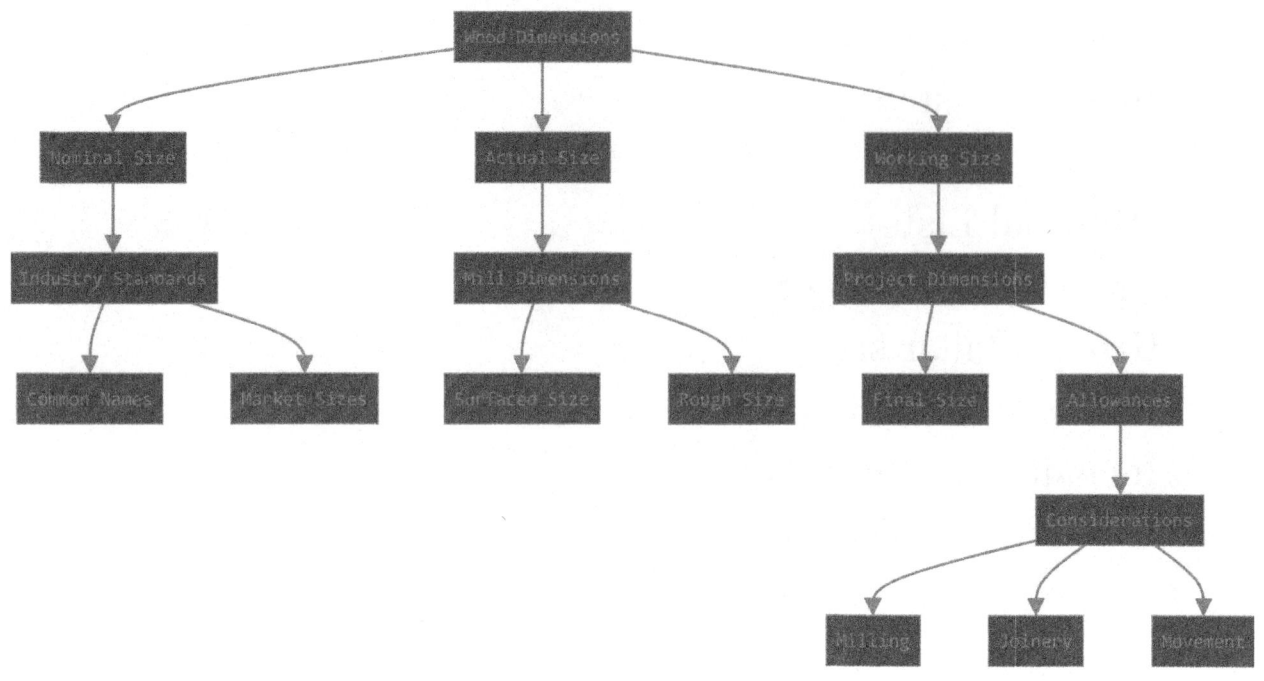

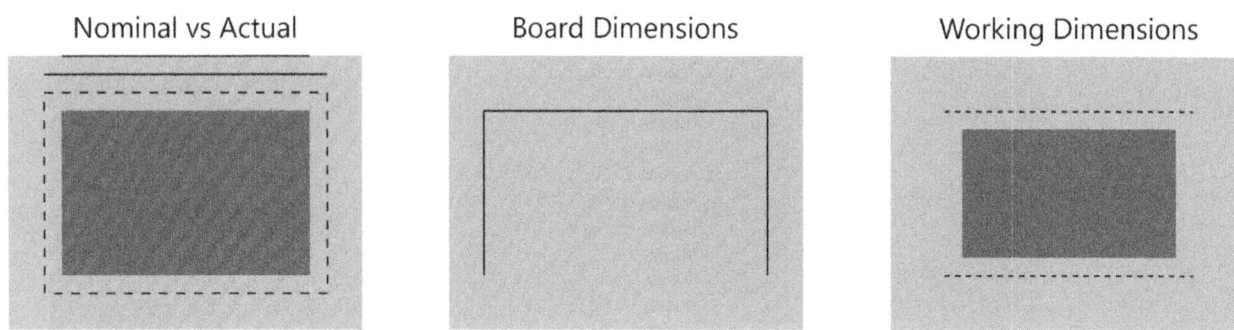

Nominal vs Actual   Board Dimensions   Working Dimensions

Marking Techniques for Accuracy

Let me guide you through the essential techniques for achieving accurate marking in woodworking. Precise marking is fundamental to quality woodworking, as even small marking errors can compound into significant problems in your finished project.

Understanding Marking Tools

Before we dive into techniques, let's understand the tools we'll be using and why each is important for specific marking tasks.

The Marking Knife

The marking knife is one of our most precise marking tools. Think of it as a surgical instrument for wood - it creates a physical incision that's both visible and tactile. Here's how to use it effectively:

1. *Proper Grip and Positioning*
   - Hold the knife at a consistent angle (around 45 degrees)
   - Keep your index finger along the blade for control
   - Position your other hand to guide the reference edge
   - Apply steady, even pressure

2. *Creating a Knife Wall*
 When we make a knife wall, we're actually creating a three-dimensional reference:
  - First cut: Light scoring to establish the line
  - Second cut: Slightly steeper angle to deepen the line
  - Third cut: Create a vertical wall by cutting at 90 degrees
  - Final result: A precise reference for saws and chisels

 The Marking Gauge
Think of the marking gauge as your parallel line artist. It transfers measurements while maintaining perfect parallelism to an edge:

1. *Setting the Gauge*
 - Clean the reference face
 - Measure carefully from the fence to the cutting point
 - Lock the setting firmly
 - Test on scrap material

2. *Making the Mark*
 - Keep constant pressure against the reference edge
 - Maintain consistent angle
 - Make multiple light passes rather than one heavy one
 - Work from left to right (if right-handed)

Essential Marking Techniques

Let's explore the fundamental techniques that ensure accuracy in your marking:

The Reference Face System
This system is like creating a GPS for your workpiece:

1. *Establishing References*
   - Choose the flattest face as Face 1
   - Mark it with a single pencil mark
   - Choose the straightest edge as Edge 1
   - Mark it with an arrow pointing to Face 1

2. *Using References*
   - All measurements start from these references
   - Keep track of your reference marks
   - Transfer measurements from these points
   - Maintain consistency throughout the project

Creating Layout Lines
Think of layout lines as your roadmap for cutting and joinery:

1. *Square Lines*
Process:
   - Position square against reference edge
   - Hold firmly in place

113

- Score with knife or draw with pencil
- Verify square from both faces

2. *Parallel Lines*
Method:
- Use marking gauge from reference edge
- Make multiple light passes
- Check spacing at multiple points
- Verify parallelism with reference

Marking for Joinery
Precise joinery requires extra attention to marking:

1. *Dovetail Layout*
Process:
- Mark baseline with gauge
- Transfer pin locations precisely
- Use dividers for consistent spacing
- Double-check all marks

2. *Mortise and Tenon*
Steps:
- Mark mortise location on stock
- Transfer to corresponding piece
- Use gauge for consistent depth
- Verify alignment marks

Verification Techniques

Always verify your marks before cutting:

1. *Measurement Verification*
Process:
- Measure from both directions
- Check against original dimensions
- Verify square or angle
- Look for obvious errors

2. *Visual Checks*
Method:
- Step back and assess overall layout
- Look for symmetry where needed
- Check reference marks
- Verify critical dimensions

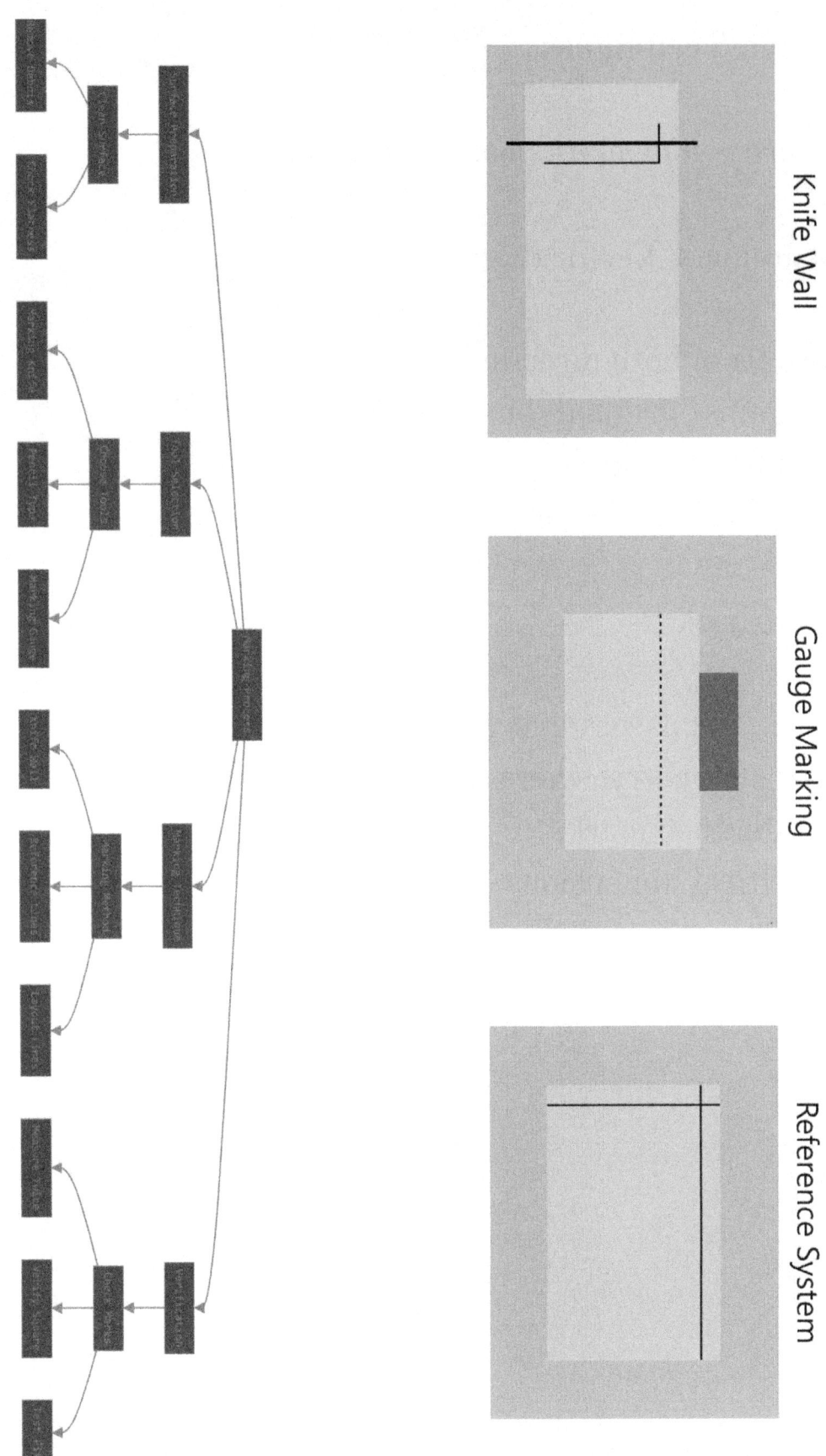

Knife Wall

Gauge Marking

Reference System

116

Creating Perfect Right Angles

Creating perfect right angles is one of the most fundamental skills in woodworking. Let me guide you through the process of achieving and verifying right angles with precision and confidence. Understanding these techniques will significantly improve the quality of your woodworking projects.

Understanding Right Angles

Before we dive into the techniques, let's understand what makes a perfect right angle and why it's so important in woodworking. A right angle is exactly 90 degrees, but achieving this precision requires both proper tools and careful technique.

The Importance of Right Angles

Right angles serve several crucial functions in woodworking:
1. They ensure parts fit together correctly
2. They maintain structural integrity
3. They create visually pleasing results
4. They allow for proper assembly of complex pieces

Essential Tools for Creating Right Angles

Let's examine the tools we'll use and how to select the right one for each task.

1. Squares

Different squares serve different purposes:

1. *Try Square*

Characteristics:
- Fixed 90-degree angle
- Wooden or metal stock
- Reference edge
- Blade length options

Usage technique:
- Hold stock firmly against reference edge
- Keep blade flat against surface
- Maintain consistent pressure
- Check for light gaps

2. *Combination Square*

Features:
- Adjustable blade
- Multiple angles
- Built-in level
- Scribing capability

Setup process:
- Clean sliding surfaces
- Lock blade securely
- Verify square setting
- Test on known square edge

Methods for Creating Right Angles

Let's explore different techniques for creating perfect right angles.

1. The Knife Wall Method

This technique creates a precise physical reference:

1. *Initial Setup*
Process:
- Clean reference edge
- Position square accurately
- Hold firmly in place
- Prepare marking knife

2. *Creating the Wall*
Steps:
- Score light line first
- Deepen with second pass
- Create vertical wall
- Verify squareness

2. The 3-4-5 Method

This ancient technique uses the Pythagorean theorem:

1. *Layout Process*
Steps:
- Mark baseline
- Measure 3 units along one edge
- Measure 4 units along perpendicular direction
- Diagonal should measure exactly 5 units

2. *Verification*
Check:
- Measure all three sides
- Verify diagonal length
- Check for consistent units
- Adjust if necessary

Verification Techniques

Always verify your right angles using multiple methods:

1. Cross Corner Method

This simple but effective technique:

1. *Process*
Steps:
- Draw perpendicular lines
- Connect opposite corners
- Measure both diagonals
- Compare measurements

2. *Analysis*
Check:
- Diagonal lengths should match
- Intersect at center point
- Equal distances from corners
- No visible discrepancies

2. Square Flip Test

A quick way to verify square accuracy:

1. *Testing Steps*
Process:
- Mark line with square
- Flip square over
- Compare lines
- Check for deviation

2. *Interpretation*
Results:
- Lines should align perfectly
- Any deviation indicates error
- Double deviation indicates square inaccuracy
- Make adjustments as needed

Common Errors and Solutions

Understanding what can go wrong helps prevent mistakes:

1. *Reference Edge Issues*
Solutions:
- True edge before marking
- Use straight edge guide
- Clean surface thoroughly
- Mark reference clearly

2. *Tool Problems*
Fixes:
- Verify tool accuracy
- Clean contact surfaces
- Check for damage
- Replace if necessary

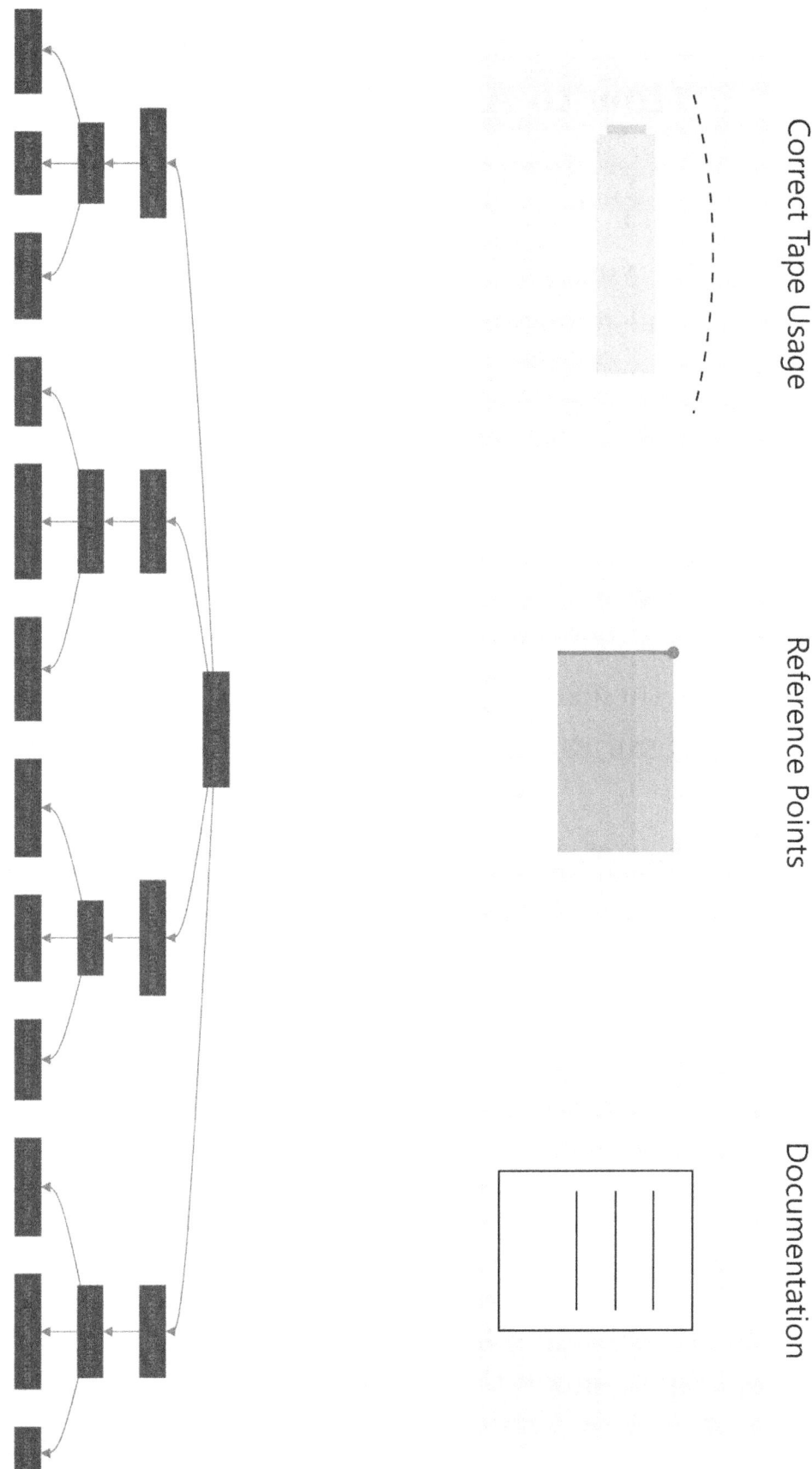

Correct Tape Usage

Reference Points

Documentation

123

Common Measuring Mistakes and How to Avoid Them

Let me guide you through the most common measuring mistakes in woodworking and explain how to avoid them. Understanding these pitfalls will help you achieve greater accuracy in your projects and reduce waste of both time and materials.

Common Tool Usage Errors

Let's begin by examining mistakes that occur with measuring tools themselves. These errors often seem small but can lead to significant problems in your finished work.

Tape Measure Errors

One of the most frequently used tools is also a common source of mistakes. Here's how to avoid tape measure errors:

1. *Hook Movement Misunderstanding*
   The sliding hook on a tape measure is intentional, but many woodworkers don't understand its purpose:
   - For outside measurements: Hook slides out
   - For inside measurements: Hook slides in
   - Movement equals hook thickness

Correct technique:
- Press hook firmly against edge for outside measurements
- Push tape body against surface for inside measurements
- Keep consistent pressure
- Verify hook movement is free but not loose

2. *Blade Sag Issues*
Long measurements can be affected by tape blade sag:
- Support the blade at regular intervals
- Use a helper for long measurements
- Consider alternative measuring methods
- Account for natural curve of tape

Square and Rule Errors

Even simple measuring tools can be sources of inaccuracy:

1. *Reference Edge Problems*
Common mistakes include:
- Not maintaining firm contact
- Allowing tool to rock
- Using damaged reference edges
- Inconsistent pressure

Solution process:
- Clean reference edges
- Check for damage
- Maintain consistent pressure

- Verify square accuracy regularly

Reference Point Errors

Many measuring mistakes stem from poor reference point selection and use.

Establishing Reference Points

1. *Reference Face System*
Proper implementation:
- Choose primary reference face
- Mark it clearly
- Use consistent marking system
- Document reference points

2. *Maintaining References*
Critical steps:
- Keep references visible
- Verify before each measurement
- Update as needed
- Document changes

Calculation Errors

Mathematical mistakes can compound quickly in woodworking.

Fraction Mathematics

1. *Common Fraction Errors*
Prevention methods:
- Use calculator when needed
- Write out calculations
- Double-check math
- Verify reasonable results

2. *Unit Conversion Mistakes*
Avoidance strategy:
- Use single measurement system
- Document conversions
- Verify calculations
- Use conversion charts

Documentation and Process Errors

Poor documentation and rushed processes lead to mistakes.

Documentation Methods

1. *Project Documentation*
Essential elements:
- Cut lists
- Dimensioned drawings
- Reference marks
- Notes and observations

2. *Measurement Recording*
Best practices:
- Use clear notation
- Include units
- Note reference points
- Record date/time

Process Improvement

1. *Verification Steps*
Implementation:
- Measure twice
- Use different tools
- Check calculations
- Verify against plans

2. *Quality Control*
System development:
- Create checklist
- Use consistent method
- Document errors
- Review and improve

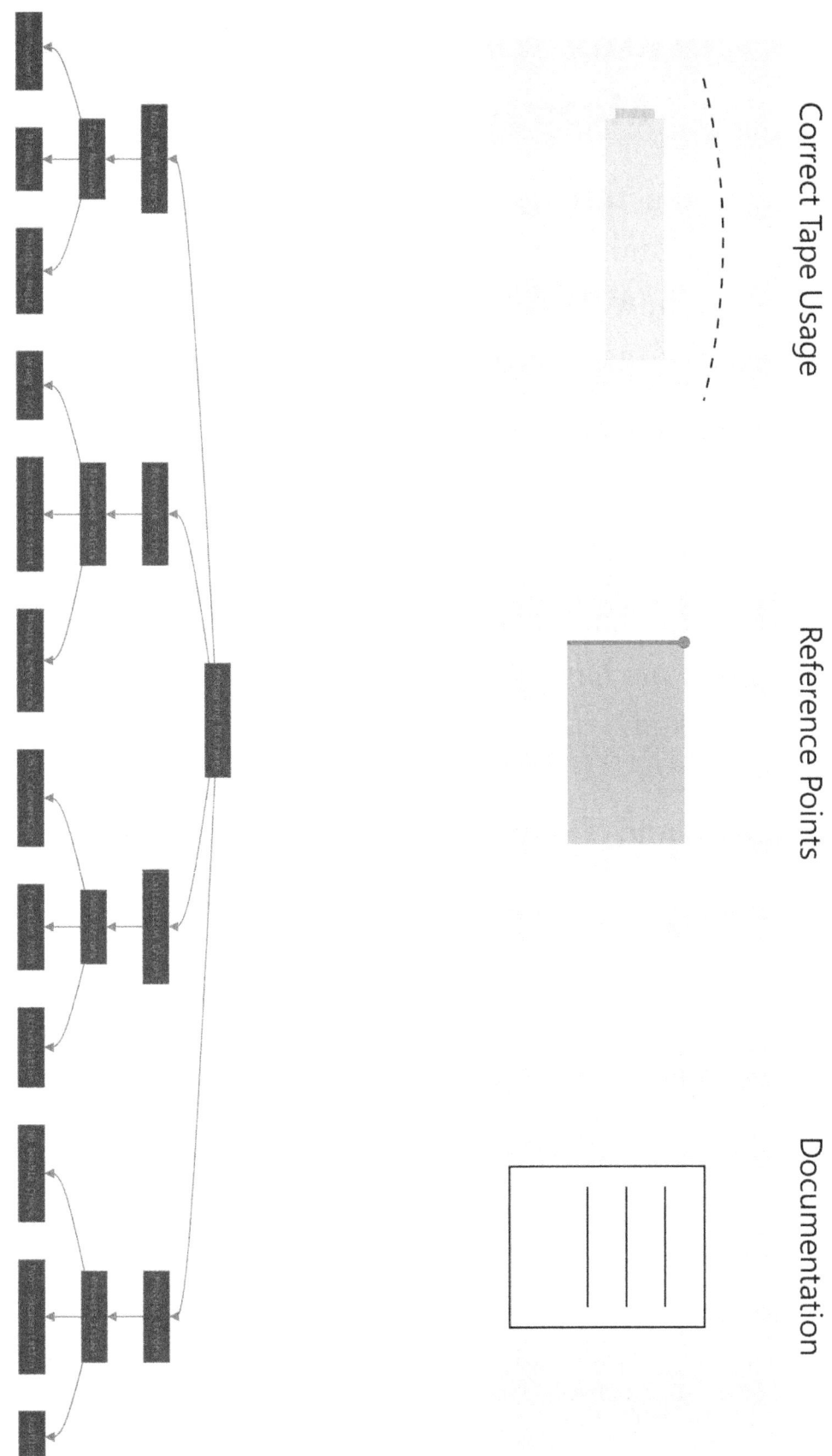

Correct Tape Usage

Reference Points

Documentation

Working with Plans and Measurements

Let me guide you through the essential process of working with plans and measurements in woodworking. Understanding how to accurately interpret and implement plans is fundamental to successful project completion.

Understanding Workshop Plans

Think of workshop plans as a detailed map for your project. Just as a map has various symbols and conventions, woodworking plans have their own language and symbols we need to understand.

Plan Elements and Their Interpretation

1. *Views and Projections*
    When you look at a plan, you'll typically see several different views of the project:
    - Top view (plan view)
    - Front view (elevation)
    - Side views
    - Detail views for complex areas

    Understanding these views requires visualizing how they relate to each other:
    - Start with the simplest view

- Compare corresponding dimensions
- Note how features align between views
- Look for hidden details

2. *Dimension Types*
Plans use different types of dimensions:
- Overall dimensions
- Detail dimensions
- Center-to-center measurements
- Clearance requirements

For each dimension, ask yourself:
- What is the reference point?
- Is this a finished dimension?
- Does it include allowances?
- How does it relate to other dimensions?

Scale Understanding and Conversion

Working with scaled plans requires careful attention to detail. Let's explore how to handle scale conversions accurately.

Working with Scale Drawings

1. *Understanding Scale Ratios*
Common woodworking scales include:
- Full scale (1:1)

- Half scale (1:2)
- Quarter scale (1:4)

To work with scales effectively:
- Write down the scale ratio
- Create a conversion chart
- Use a scale ruler if available
- Double-check all conversions

2. *Converting Measurements*
When converting scaled measurements:
- Use consistent units
- Write out calculations
- Verify reasonable results
- Document conversions

Measurement Transfer Methods

Transferring measurements from plans to your work requires reliable methods.

Story Stick Method

Think of a story stick as a full-scale template of your measurements:

1. *Creating a Story Stick*
Process:
- Select straight, stable material
- Mark reference edge clearly
- Transfer measurements directly
- Label each mark clearly

Benefits:
- Eliminates conversion errors
- Provides consistent reference
- Easy to duplicate measurements
- Preserves original dimensions

Template Creation

Templates are especially useful for complex or repeated shapes:

1. *Making Accurate Templates*
Steps:
- Transfer dimensions carefully
- Include alignment marks
- Note grain direction
- Mark reference edges

Usage:
- Test fit before cutting
- Check for symmetry

133

- Verify all dimensions
- Document any adjustments

Implementation Strategies

Putting plans into practice requires a systematic approach.

Layout Process

1. *Material Preparation*
Before marking:
- True reference edges
- Clean surfaces
- Check for defects
- Plan grain orientation

2. *Marking Sequence*
Systematic approach:
- Start with reference lines
- Work from large to small
- Double-check measurements
- Mark cutting allowances

Error Prevention

Develop habits that prevent mistakes:

1. *Verification Steps*
Create a routine:
- Check measurements twice
- Verify against plans
- Test critical fits
- Document changes

2. *Documentation*
Keep records of:
- Plan modifications
- Actual measurements
- Problem areas
- Solutions implemented

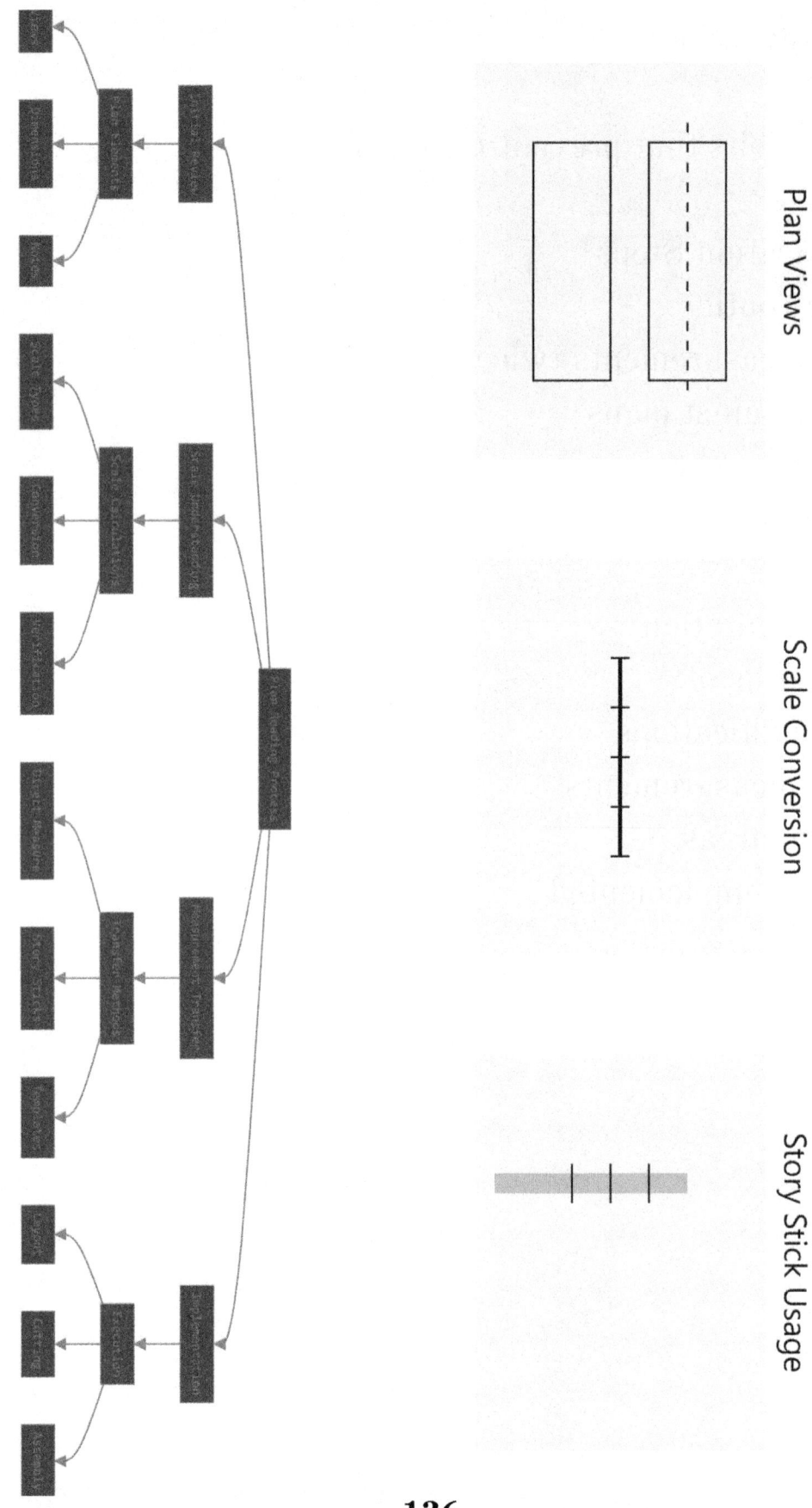

Plan Views

Scale Conversion

Story Stick Usage

136

Chapter 4
Reading and Understanding Woodworking Plans

Anatomy of a Woodworking Plan

Let me walk you through understanding the essential components of a woodworking plan. Think of a woodworking plan as a detailed map that guides you through your project, where each element serves a specific purpose in communicating important information.

Understanding Title Information

The title block is your plan's introduction. Just as a book's cover gives you essential information about its contents, the title block provides crucial details about your project.

Elements of the Title Block

1. *Project Identification*
   Think of this as your project's birth certificate. It includes:
   - Project name and description
   - Drawing number or reference
   - Date of creation
   - Revision information
   - Designer's name

Look for:
- Clear, specific project titles
- Current revision numbers
- Date of last update
- Any special notes

Scale Information

2. *Scale Notation*
This tells you how the drawing relates to actual size:
- Written as ratios (1:1, 1:2, etc.)
- May include scale bars
- Multiple scales for different views
- Scale references

Understanding scales:
- 1:1 means actual size
- 1:2 means half size
- 2:1 means double size
- Always verify scale before measuring

Views and Projections

Think of views as different camera angles of your project. Each view reveals different aspects of the design.

Types of Views

1. *Orthographic Projections*
These are like looking at a box from different sides:
- Front elevation (front view)
- Side elevation (side view)
- Plan view (top view)
- Rear elevation (back view)

How to read them:
- Start with the simplest view
- Compare related dimensions
- Note how features align
- Look for hidden lines

2. *Section Views*
These show what you'd see if you cut through the project:
- Called out by section lines
- Show internal construction
- Reveal joinery details
- Indicate material thickness

Reading sections:
- Follow cutting plane line
- Note direction of view
- Understand material symbols
- Check dimensional relationships

Dimensions and Notes

Dimensions are the numerical language of your plan. They provide the exact measurements needed to build the project.

Understanding Dimension Types

1. *Linear Dimensions*
These show straight-line measurements:
- Overall dimensions
- Detail dimensions
- Spacing dimensions
- Clearance requirements

How to read them:
- Start with largest dimensions
- Work down to details
- Cross-reference between views
- Note any tolerances

2. *Angular Dimensions*
These show angles and slopes:
- Degrees of angle
- Slope ratios
- Tapers
- Bevels

Reading angles:
- Note measurement units
- Check reference faces
- Verify complementary angles
- Consider tool setup

Technical Details

These provide specific information about materials, construction, and assembly.

Material Specifications

1. *Material Callouts*
These indicate what materials to use:
- Wood species
- Grade requirements
- Special treatments
- Finish specifications

Understanding specifications:
- Check material availability
- Note grain requirements
- Consider alternatives
- Verify compatibility

2. *Hardware Requirements*
Details about fasteners and fittings:
- Screw sizes and types
- Hinges and hardware
- Specialty fittings
- Quantity requirements

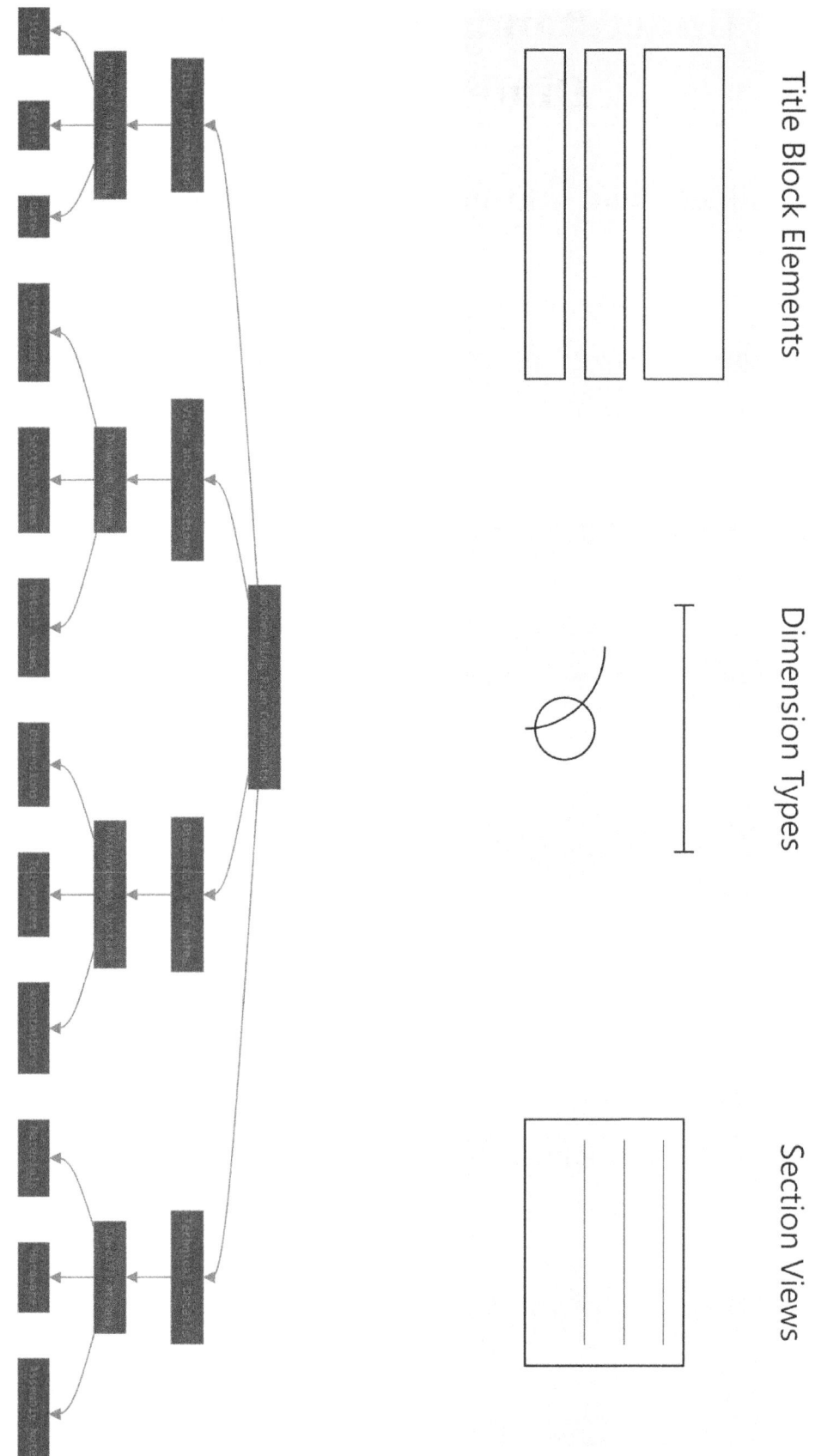

Title Block Elements

Dimension Types

Section Views

Understanding Scale and Dimensions

Let me guide you through the essential concepts of understanding scale and dimensions in woodworking plans. Think of scale as a consistent way to represent large objects in a manageable size, much like how maps represent vast distances on a single page.

Understanding Scale Fundamentals

Scale is a mathematical relationship between the size of something on paper and its actual size. Let's break this down into manageable concepts.

Basic Scale Ratios

When we work with scale, we're essentially using a form of proportion. The most common scales you'll encounter are:

1. *Full Scale (1:1)*
   - Actual size representation
   - One unit on paper equals one unit in reality
   - Used for detail drawings and full-sized templates

Example calculation:
```

If a line measures 3 inches on the drawing at 1:1
Actual size = 3 inches × 1 = 3 inches
```


2. *Half Scale (1:2)*
 - Half of actual size
 - Two units in reality equal one unit on paper
 - Common for medium-sized projects

Example calculation:
```

If a line measures 3 inches on the drawing at 1:2
Actual size = 3 inches × 2 = 6 inches
```


Scale Conversion Process

Learning to convert between scales is crucial. Here's a systematic approach:

1. *Identify the Scale*
Steps:
 - Look for scale notation
 - Check title block
 - Verify with known dimensions
 - Note any varying scales

2. *Convert Measurements*
Process:
- Write down the measurement
- Identify the scale ratio
- Multiply by scale factor
- Verify reasonableness

Working with Different Measurement Systems

Understanding both imperial and metric measurements is essential in modern woodworking.

Imperial System

1. *Fractional Measurements*
Working process:
- Convert to smallest common denominator
- Add measurements carefully
- Double-check calculations
- Consider using decimal equivalents

Example:
```

3/4" + 5/8" = 6/8" + 5/8" = 11/8" = 1-3/8"
```

2. *Decimal Conversions*
Useful for:
- Complex calculations
- Machine settings
- Precise measurements
- Digital tool use

Metric System

1. *Basic Units*
Understanding:
- Millimeters (mm) - most common
- Centimeters (cm) - less common
- Meters (m) - large projects

Conversion tips:
- Work in one unit consistently
- Avoid mixing units
- Use decimal points carefully

Scale Drawing Tools and Techniques

Using the right tools makes scale work easier:

1. Architect's Scale
Features:
- Multiple scales on one tool
- Built-in conversions

- Precise measurements
- Easy to read

Usage technique:
1. Select correct scale
2. Align zero point
3. Read measurement
4. Verify scale factor

2. Digital Calipers
Benefits:
- Switch between systems
- Precise readings
- Digital display
- Zero reset capability

Usage steps:
1. Zero the tool
2. Take measurement
3. Convert if needed
4. Record result

Common Scale Errors and Prevention

Understanding common mistakes helps avoid them:

1. Scale Confusion

Prevention steps:

- Mark scale on all drawings
- Use consistent scales
- Double-check calculations
- Maintain clear notes

2. Measurement Errors

Avoiding mistakes:

- Use appropriate tools
- Verify measurements
- Document clearly
- Check calculations

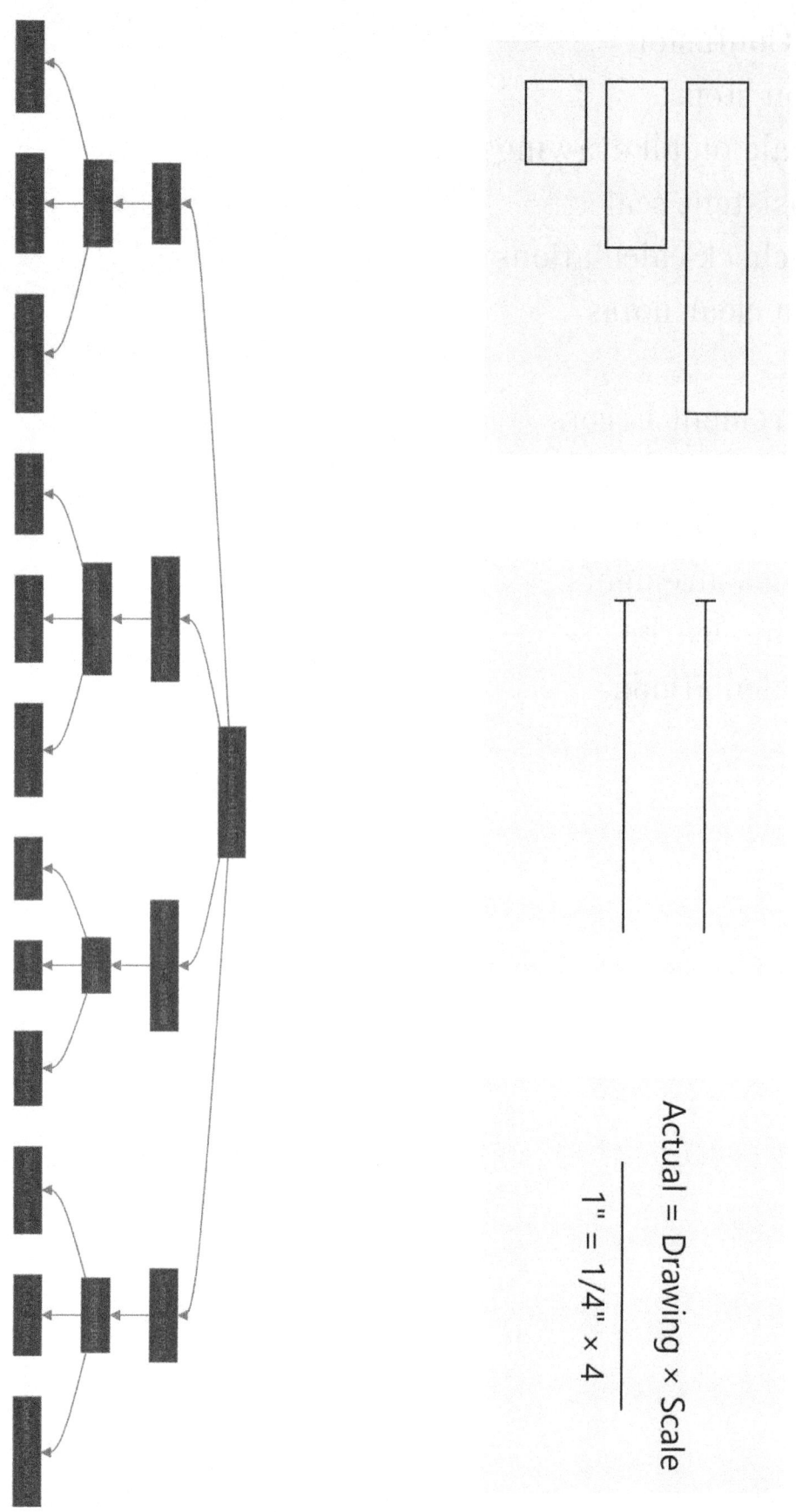

Scale Comparison

Measurement Systems

Scale Calculation

$$\text{Actual} = \text{Drawing} \times \text{Scale}$$

$$1" = 1/4" \times 4$$

Reading Technical Drawings

Let me guide you through the process of reading and understanding technical drawings in woodworking. Think of technical drawings as a universal language that communicates all the information needed to build a project. Just as learning any language, understanding technical drawings requires familiarity with its vocabulary and grammar.

Understanding Line Types

In technical drawings, different types of lines convey different meanings. Think of these lines as the basic vocabulary of technical drawings.

Basic Line Types and Their Meanings

1. *Object Lines (Solid Lines)*
   These represent visible edges and surfaces:
   - Draw with bold, solid lines
   - Show what you can see directly
   - Represent outer edges
   - Define visible boundaries

   How to interpret:
   - Follow solid lines first
   - Note where they intersect

- Understand their relationships
- Visualize the 3D form

2. *Hidden Lines (Dashed)*
These show edges that exist but aren't visible:
- Drawn as evenly spaced dashes
- Represent concealed features
- Show internal construction
- Aid in understanding structure

Reading technique:
- Imagine looking through material
- Connect to visible features
- Understand spatial relationships
- Verify against other views

Understanding Views

Technical drawings typically show multiple views of the same object. Think of these as different camera angles that work together to tell the complete story.

Orthographic Projections

1. *Front View (Elevation)*
This is like looking straight at the project:
- Shows height and width
- Primary view for most projects

- Reference for other views
- Contains main dimensions

Analysis process:
- Start with overall dimensions
- Note major features
- Look for symmetry
- Check proportions

2. *Top View (Plan)*
Looking down from above:
- Shows length and width
- Reveals layout patterns
- Important for joinery
- Shows material orientation

Section Views

Think of section views as cutting through the project to reveal internal details:

1. *Creating Mental Images*
Process:
- Identify cutting plane line
- Visualize the cut
- Note material symbols
- Understand internal structure

Understanding technique:
- Follow cutting line
- Note direction arrows
- Study revealed details
- Connect to other views

Dimension Reading

Dimensions provide the exact measurements needed for construction:

Types of Dimensions

1. *Linear Dimensions*
Basic measurements:
- Overall dimensions
- Detail dimensions
- Location dimensions
- Clearance requirements

Reading process:
- Start with largest dimensions
- Work to smaller details
- Verify relationships
- Check for completeness

2. *Angular Dimensions*
Show angles and slopes:
- Degree measurements
- Slope ratios
- Bevel angles
- Compound angles

Understanding process:
- Note measurement type
- Check reference edges
- Consider tool setup
- Verify feasibility

Drawing Annotations

Additional information beyond lines and dimensions:

Types of Notes

1. *General Notes*
Overall project information:
- Material specifications
- Finish requirements
- Assembly instructions
- Special considerations

How to use:
- Read all notes first
- Mark critical information
- Cross-reference with views
- Document questions

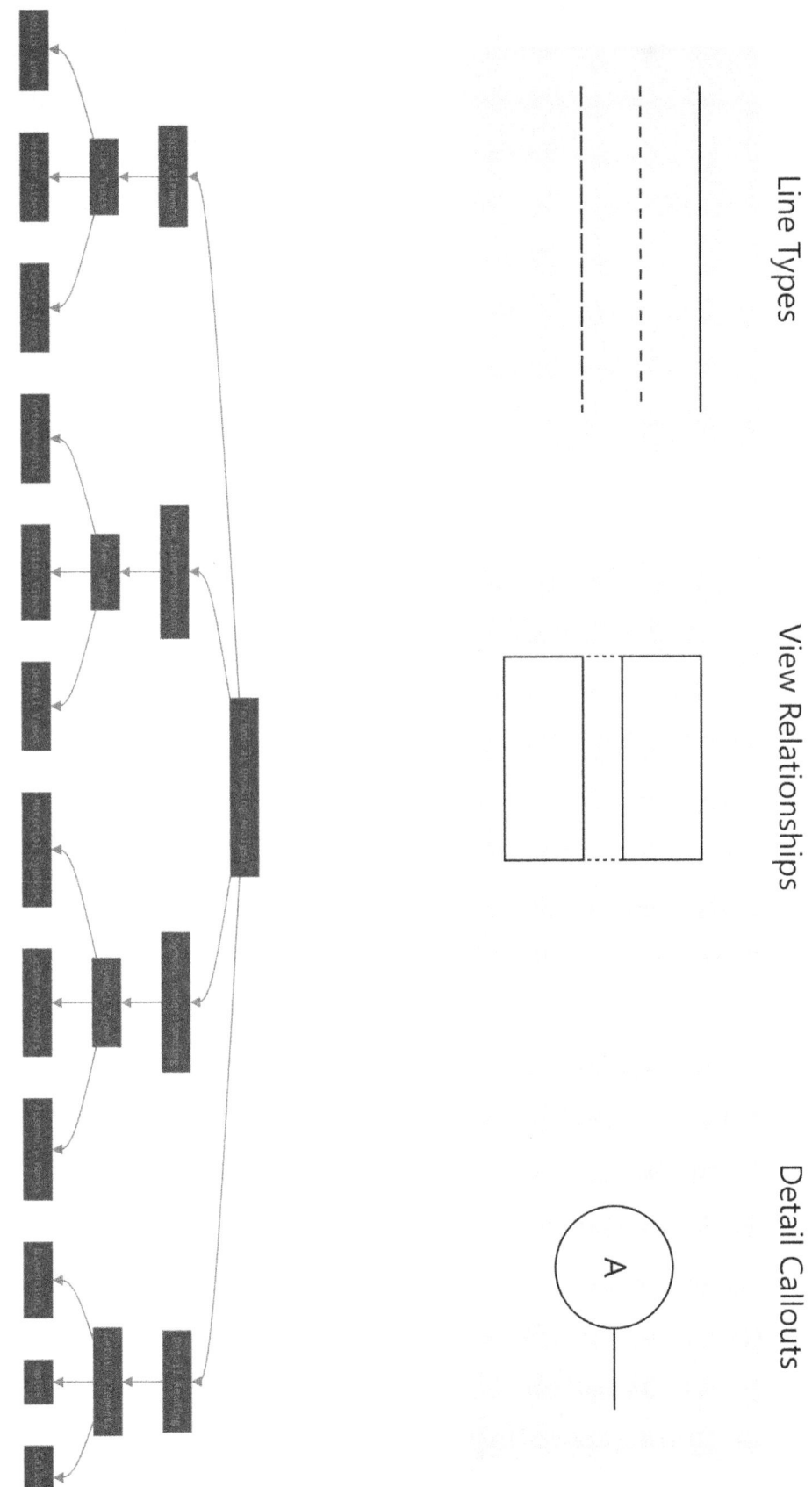

Line Types

View Relationships

Detail Callouts

A

Creating Your Own Simple Plans

Let me guide you through the process of creating your own woodworking plans, starting from initial concept to final documentation. Creating plans is like writing a story about your project before you build it, ensuring that every detail is thought through and clearly communicated.

Initial Concept Development

The first phase of plan creation involves transforming your ideas into initial sketches and basic measurements.

Starting with Sketches

Think of sketches as your project's rough draft. Begin with:

1. *Basic Shape Development*
   Process:
   - Start with simple shapes
   - Use grid paper for proportion
   - Sketch multiple views
   - Add basic dimensions

   Technique:
   - Keep lines light initially
   - Use basic geometric shapes
   - Focus on proportions

- Don't worry about perfection

2. *Preliminary Dimensions*
Consider:
- Overall size requirements
- Material limitations
- Space constraints
- Practical usage

Layout Development

Once you have basic sketches, move to more formal layout:

Creating Basic Views

1. *Orthographic Projections*
Start with three main views:
- Front elevation (front view)
- Top view (plan view)
- Side elevation (end view)

Drawing process:
- Begin with largest view
- Maintain proportions
- Project lines between views
- Keep views aligned

2. *View Arrangement*
Organization tips:
- Leave space between views
- Plan for dimensions
- Consider note placement
- Allow for title block

Adding Details

With basic views established, add construction details:

Joinery Details

1. *Joint Representation*
Show:
- Joint types
- Dimensions
- Assembly sequence
- Special considerations

Drawing method:
- Use standard symbols
- Show hidden lines
- Include critical dimensions
- Add explanatory notes

2. *Hardware Specifications*
Document:
- Type and size
- Location
- Quantity
- Installation notes

Dimensioning Your Plans

Proper dimensioning is crucial for clarity:

Dimension Placement

1. *Basic Rules*
Follow these guidelines:
- Place dimensions outside views
- Use consistent spacing
- Group related dimensions
- Avoid crossing lines

Implementation:
- Start with overall dimensions
- Add detail dimensions
- Check for completeness
- Verify accuracy

2. *Dimension Types*
Include:
- Overall dimensions
- Detail dimensions
- Location dimensions
- Assembly dimensions

Creating Supporting Documentation

Complete your plans with additional information:

Materials List

1. *Components List*
Include:
- Part names
- Quantities
- Dimensions
- Materials

Organization:
- Group similar items
- List in logical order
- Include stock sizes
- Note special requirements

2. *Construction Notes*
Document:
- Assembly sequence
- Special techniques
- Finish requirements
- Safety considerations

Final Checks and Verification

Before considering plans complete:

Quality Control

1. *Verification Steps*
Check:
- All dimensions present
- Views consistent
- Notes complete
- Scale accurate

Process:
- Review systematically
- Check calculations
- Verify measurements
- Test readability

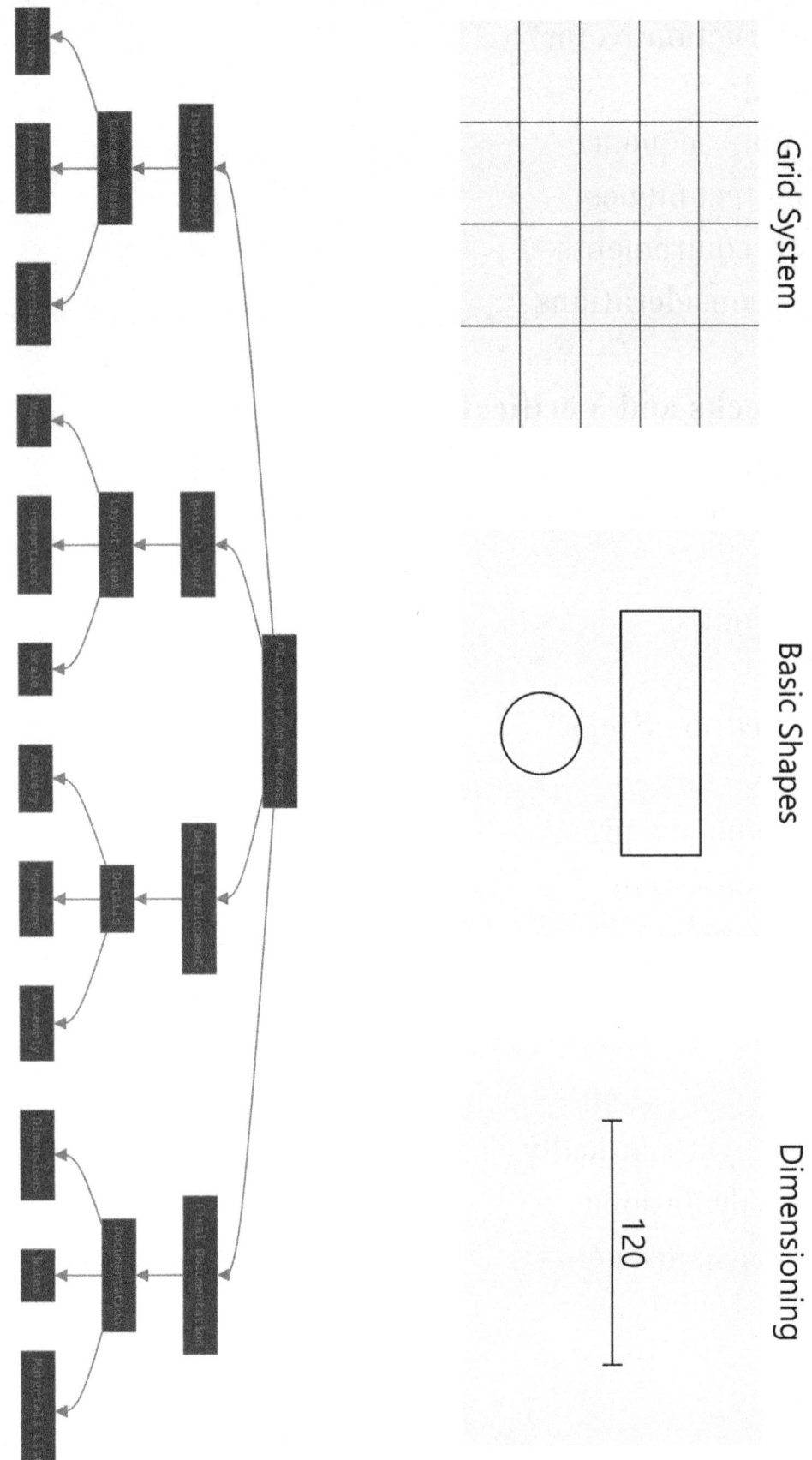

Grid System

Basic Shapes

Dimensioning

120

164

Converting Measurements and Scaling Projects

Let me guide you through the essential process of converting measurements and scaling projects. This fundamental skill allows you to adapt plans to your needs while maintaining proper proportions. Think of it as learning to translate between different languages of measurement while keeping the original meaning intact.

Understanding Measurement Systems

Before we dive into conversion, let's establish a solid understanding of the measurement systems we'll be working with. This foundation is crucial for accurate conversions.

Imperial System Fundamentals

The imperial system is built on inches and feet, but its true complexity lies in fractional measurements:

1. *Fractions in Woodworking*
   Common fractions you'll encounter:
   - Halves (1/2")
   - Quarters (1/4")
   - Eighths (1/8")
   - Sixteenths (1/16")

Important concept: All these fractions relate to one inch as the whole unit. To convert between them:

```
1/2" = 8/16"
1/4" = 4/16"
3/8" = 6/16"
```

2. *Decimal Equivalents*
Converting fractions to decimals makes calculations easier:
- 1/2" = 0.500"
- 1/4" = 0.250"
- 1/8" = 0.125"
- 1/16" = 0.0625"

Metric System Understanding

The metric system is based on units of 10, making it inherently simpler for calculations:

1. *Common Units*
In woodworking, we primarily use:
- Millimeters (mm) - most common
- Centimeters (cm) - for rough measurements
- Meters (m) - for very large projects

Converting between metric units:
```

1 meter = 100 centimeters = 1000 millimeters
1 centimeter = 10 millimeters
```

Conversion Between Systems

Now let's explore how to convert between imperial and metric measurements accurately.

Basic Conversion Formulas

The fundamental conversion factors:
1. *Inches to Millimeters*
```

1 inch = 25.4 millimeters
```

To convert:
- Multiply inches by 25.4 for millimeters
- For fractions, convert to decimal first
- Round to nearest millimeter for practicality

2. *Millimeters to Inches*
```

1 millimeter = 0.03937 inches
```

Process:
- Divide millimeters by 25.4 for inches
- Convert decimal to nearest practical fraction
- Use common fractions when possible

Scaling Projects

Scaling involves changing the size of a project while maintaining its proportions.

Understanding Scale Ratios

1. *Common Scale Ratios*
Typical woodworking scales:
- Full scale (1:1)
- Half scale (1:2)
- Quarter scale (1:4)

How to read ratios:
- First number is drawing measurement
- Second number is actual measurement
- Example: 1:2 means 1 inch on paper = 2 inches actual size

2. *Scaling Calculations*
To scale measurements:
```

Actual size = Drawing measurement × Scale factor
```

Example:
- If drawing shows 3" at 1:2 scale
- Actual size = 3" × 2 = 6"

Proportional Scaling

When changing project size:

1. *Maintaining Proportions*
Process:
- Determine scale factor
- Apply to all dimensions
- Check critical measurements
- Adjust for material limitations

Example calculation:
```

Original size: 24" × 36"
Scale factor: 0.75
New size: 18" × 27"
```

2. *Critical Considerations*
When scaling, check:
- Material thickness ratios
- Joint proportions
- Hardware compatibility
- Structural integrity

Practical Tips for Accuracy

Ensure accuracy in your conversions and scaling:

Double-Check Methods

1. *Cross-Verification*
Always:
- Calculate both ways
- Use different tools
- Compare results
- Document calculations

2. *Common Sense Check*
Ask yourself:
- Does this measurement make sense?
- Is it practical?
- Will it work with standard materials?
- Does it meet project needs?

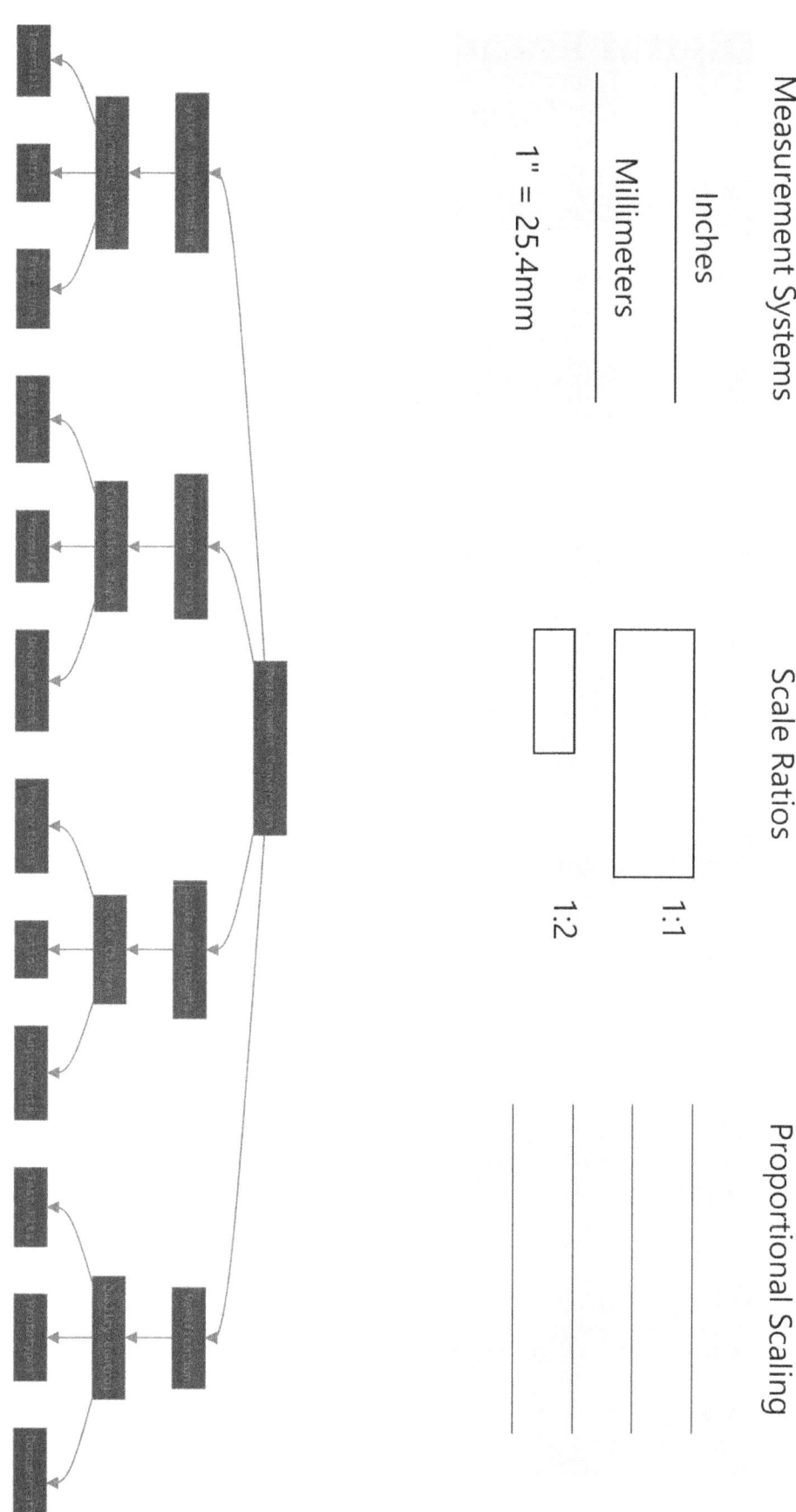

Measurement Systems

Inches

Millimeters

1" = 25.4mm

Scale Ratios

1:1

1:2

Proportional Scaling

Digital Planning Tools and Resources

Let me guide you through the world of digital planning tools and resources for woodworking. Think of these tools as your digital workshop, where each application serves a specific purpose in bringing your projects from concept to completion.

Understanding CAD Software Options

Computer-Aided Design (CAD) software forms the foundation of digital woodworking planning. Let's explore the different types and their applications.

Entry-Level CAD Software

When you're beginning with digital planning, start with user-friendly options:

1. *SketchUp Free*
   Features and usage:
   - Web-based interface
   - Basic 3D modeling
   - Extensive component library
   - Free to use

Getting started:
- Create account
- Complete basic tutorials
- Start with simple projects
- Use woodworking templates

2. *FreeCAD*
Capabilities:
- Open-source
- Parametric modeling
- 2D drafting
- 3D design

Learning process:
- Install software
- Follow workbench tutorials
- Practice basic commands
- Join user community

Specialized Woodworking Software

These tools are designed specifically for woodworking projects:

Design and Planning Tools

1. *Cabinet Planner Software*
Features:
- Standard cabinet sizes
- Material calculations
- Cut lists generation
- Hardware specification

Implementation:
- Input project dimensions
- Select cabinet styles
- Customize components
- Generate materials list

2. *Cut List Optimizers*
Functionality:
- Material optimization
- Waste reduction
- Cost calculation
- Layout visualization

Usage process:
- Enter material sizes
- Input required pieces
- Set grain direction
- Generate cutting plans

Mobile Applications

Mobile apps can enhance your workshop efficiency:

Measurement and Calculation Apps

1. *Digital Measuring Tools*
Applications:
- Room measurements
- Angle finding
- Level checking
- Photo measurements

Best practices:
- Calibrate tools
- Take multiple measurements
- Save results
- Cross-reference

2. *Woodworking Calculators*
Features:
- Board foot calculation
- Joint sizing
- Material estimation
- Project costing

Usage:
- Input dimensions
- Select material type
- Calculate quantities
- Save calculations

Project Management Tools

Organizing your woodworking projects digitally:

Planning and Tracking

1. *Project Timeline Tools*
Features:
- Task scheduling
- Progress tracking
- Material ordering
- Deadline management

Implementation:
- Create project timeline
- Set milestones
- Track progress
- Update regularly

2. *Cost Tracking Software*
Capabilities:
- Material costs

- Time tracking
- Expense recording
- Budget comparison

Process:
- Set up project budget
- Record expenses
- Track labor time
- Generate reports

Online Resources and Communities

Leveraging digital resources for knowledge and support:

Online Woodworking Communities

1. *Forums and Discussion Boards*
Benefits:
- Expert advice
- Project sharing
- Problem solving
- Technique discussion

Participation:
- Create profile
- Read guidelines
- Share projects
- Ask questions

2. *Video Tutorial Platforms*
Resources:
- Technique demonstrations
- Project walkthroughs
- Tool reviews
- Tips and tricks

Learning approach:
- Start with basics
- Follow along with projects
- Take notes
- Practice techniques

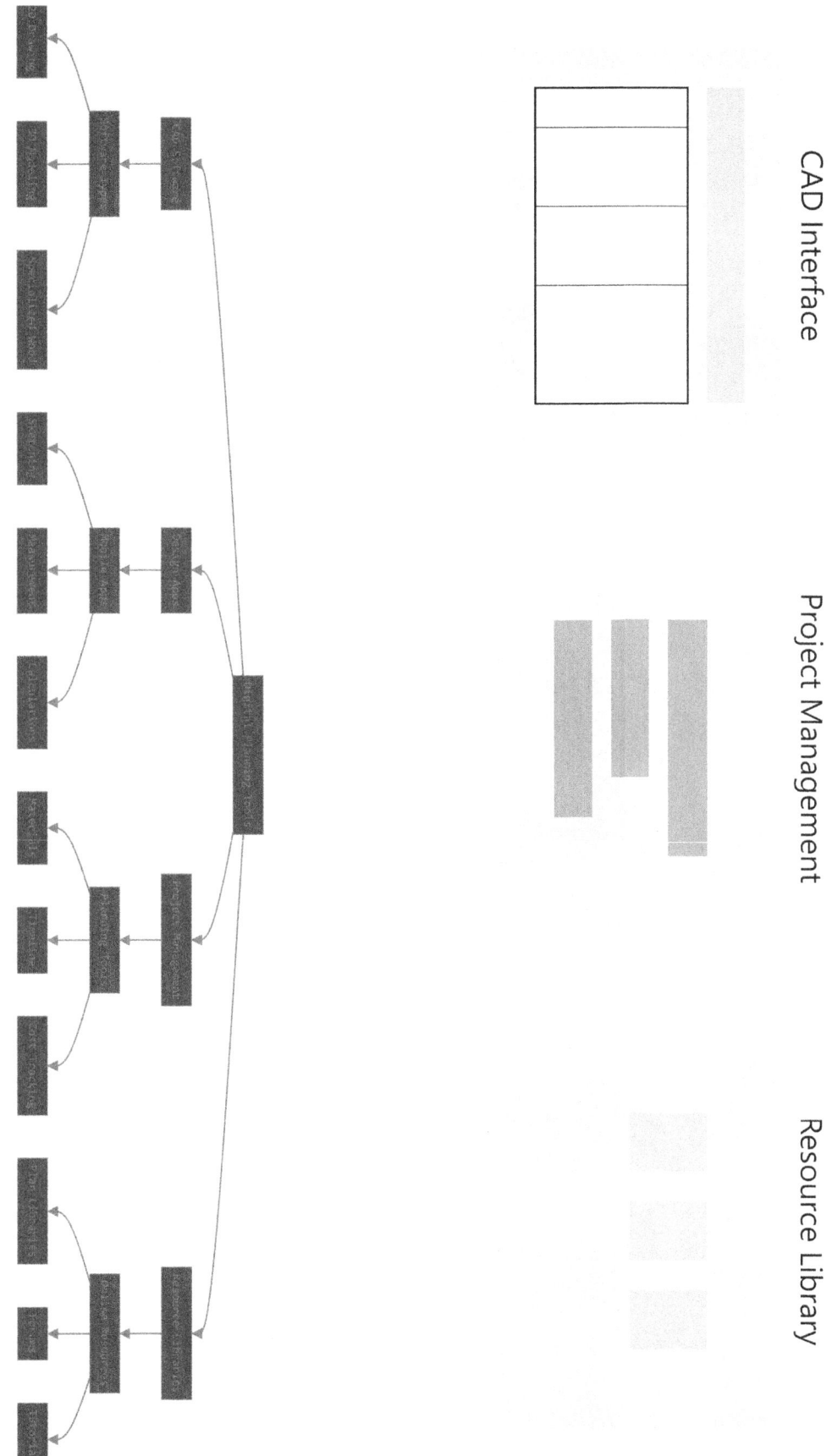

CAD Interface

Project Management

Resource Library

179

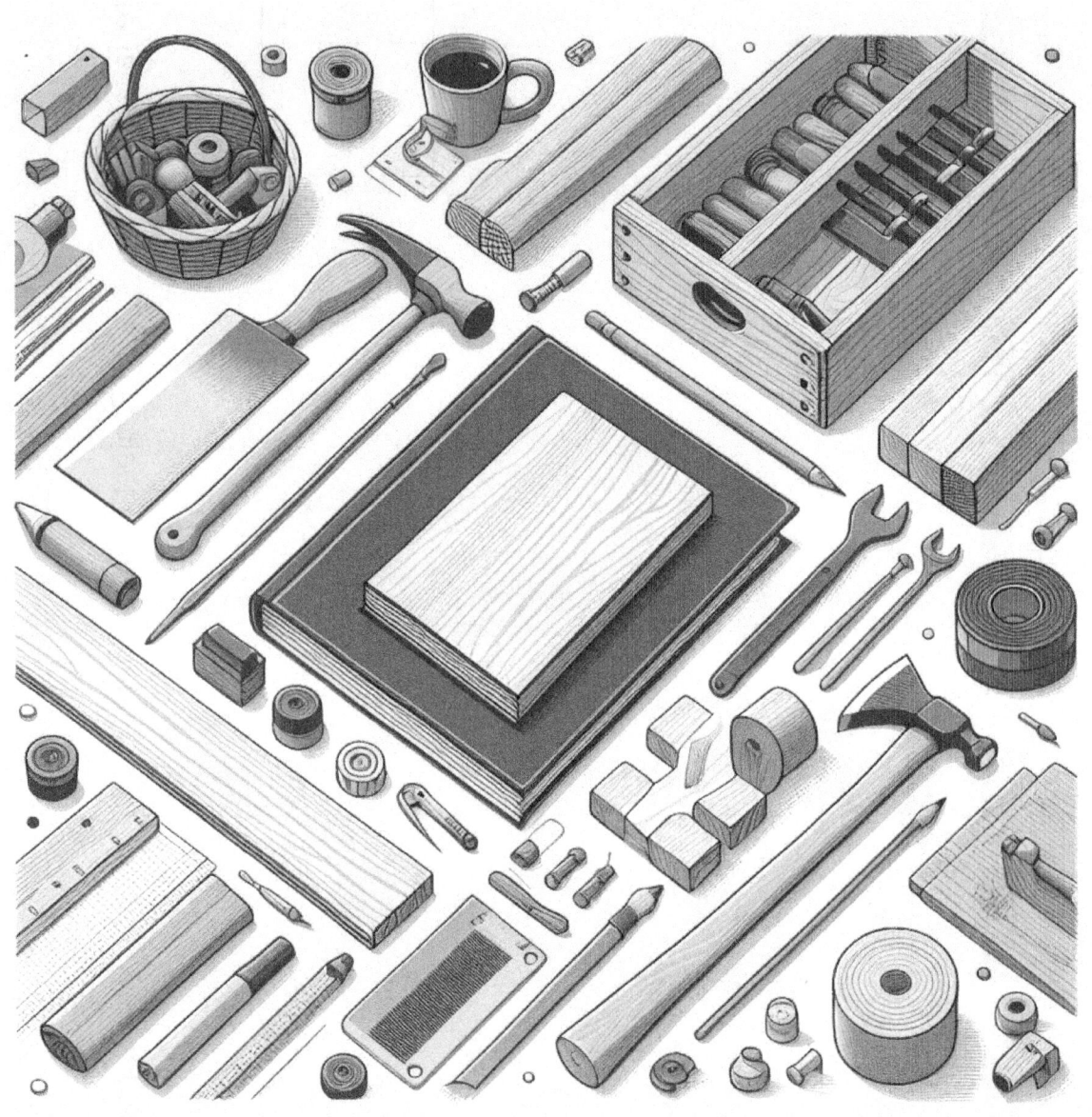

Chapter 5
Basic Woodworking Techniques

Cutting Techniques and Best Practices

Let me guide you through the essential techniques and best practices for cutting wood effectively and safely. Think of cutting as the foundation of woodworking – just as a chef needs to master knife skills, a woodworker must understand the art of making precise cuts.

Understanding Basic Cutting Principles

Before we dive into specific techniques, it's important to understand the fundamental principles that govern all wood cutting. Think of wood grain as a bundle of straws – the direction in which you cut relative to these "straws" dramatically affects your results.

The Nature of Wood Grain

When we cut wood, we're dealing with two primary grain orientations:

1. *With the grain (ripping)*
 - Like splitting the bundle of straws lengthwise
 - Requires less force but more control
 - Creates long, stringy waste
 - Follows wood's natural separation lines

2. *Across the grain (crosscutting)*
 - Like cutting across the bundle of straws
 - Requires more force but easier to control
 - Creates shorter, chip-like waste
 - Needs more support to prevent tearout

Hand Saw Techniques

Let's explore the proper techniques for using hand saws, starting with the basics and building to more advanced skills.

Proper Grip and Stance

Think of your sawing stance as similar to a martial artist's stance – it provides balance, control, and power:

1. *Hand Position*
Proper grip technique:
 - Wrap fingers around handle naturally
 - Keep thumb along handle top
 - Maintain relaxed but firm grip
 - Allow saw to pivot slightly

Common mistakes to avoid:
- Gripping too tightly
- Forcing the saw
- Using incorrect angle
- Poor wrist position

2. *Body Position*
Optimal stance:
- Stand at 45° angle to work
- Keep feet shoulder-width apart
- Align shoulder with cutting line
- Maintain comfortable posture

Starting the Cut

The beginning of the cut is crucial for accuracy:

1. *Creating a Starting Notch*
Process:
- Score line with knife
- Make shallow backward strokes
- Use thumb as guide
- Gradually deepen cut

Key points:
- Light pressure initially
- Keep saw vertical
- Watch cutting line

- Feel for smoothness

Advanced Cutting Techniques

Once you've mastered the basics, you can move on to more sophisticated cutting methods.

Precision Crosscuts

For accurate crosscuts across the grain:

1. *Setup Process*
Steps:
- Mark cutting line clearly
- Support both sides of cut
- Position waste side properly
- Check square alignment

Verification:
- Measure twice
- Check square
- Verify support
- Test lighting

2. *Cutting Sequence*
Execution:
- Start with back corner
- Use full blade length

- Maintain steady rhythm
- Complete cut smoothly

Rip Cuts Along Grain

For cutting with the grain:

1. *Preparation*
Requirements:
- Straight reference edge
- Adequate support
- Clear cutting line
- Proper lighting

Setup process:
- Secure workpiece
- Mark waste side
- Check grain direction
- Position supports

2. *Execution*
Technique:
- Begin at far end
- Use shallow angle
- Follow grain direction
- Maintain steady pressure

Safety Considerations

Safety must always be your first priority:

Personal Protection

1. *Essential Safety Gear*
Required items:
- Safety glasses
- Hearing protection
- Dust mask when needed
- Appropriate clothing

Usage:
- Wear before starting
- Check fit and function
- Maintain clean condition
- Replace as needed

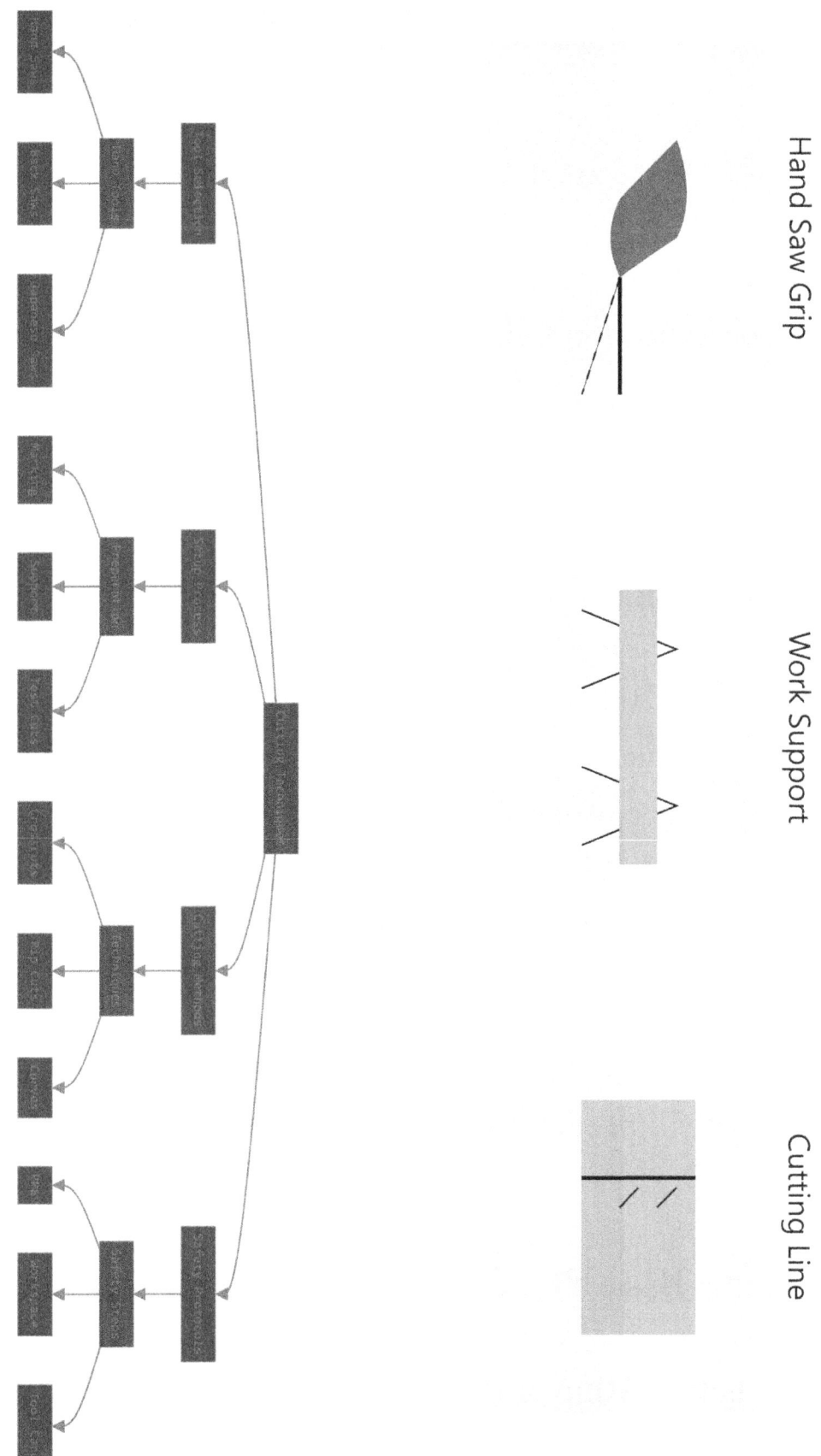

Hand Saw Grip

Work Support

Cutting Line

Joining Wood: Basic Methods

When we join pieces of wood together, we're creating connections that must not only be strong but also accommodate the natural movement of wood over time. Think of wood joinery as a language of connections, where each type of joint tells a different story about how the pieces work together. Let me walk you through the fundamental methods of joining wood, explaining not just what to do, but why we do it.

Understanding Basic Joint Types

Let's begin with the most fundamental joints that form the foundation of woodworking. Think of these as the alphabet of wood joinery – simple elements that combine to create more complex structures.

The Butt Joint

The butt joint is the simplest form of wood connection, but understanding it properly sets the stage for more complex joinery:

1. *Creating a Basic Butt Joint*
   Process:
   - Square both mating surfaces perfectly
   - Check for tight fit across entire surface

- Mark mating faces for reference
- Prepare surfaces for glue

Critical considerations:
- Surface flatness affects strength
- End grain requires special preparation
- Consider grain direction
- Plan for wood movement

2. *Reinforcing Butt Joints*
Methods to strengthen:
- Add glue blocks for support
- Use mechanical fasteners
- Apply splines or biscuits
- Consider corner blocks

The Rabbet Joint

A step up from the butt joint, the rabbet creates a mechanical connection while maintaining simplicity:

1. *Cutting a Rabbet*
Step-by-step process:
- Mark rabbet dimensions clearly
- Set up cutting tools precisely
- Make test cuts on scrap
- Cut in multiple passes

Key measurements:
- Depth typically 1/3 material thickness
- Width based on mating piece
- Allow for wood movement
- Consider final appearance

Advanced Joinery Methods

As we progress to more sophisticated joints, we'll explore techniques that provide both strength and beauty.

Mortise and Tenon Joints

This classic joint has stood the test of time for good reason:

1. *Layout Process*
Careful marking is essential:
- Mark mortise position precisely
- Transfer marks to tenon piece
- Include offset for wood movement
- Mark waste areas clearly

Layout tools needed:
- Marking gauge
- Square
- Mortise gauge
- Sharp pencil or knife

2. *Cutting the Joint*
Sequence matters:
- Cut mortise first
- Size tenon to fit
- Test fit frequently
- Adjust as needed

Assembly Techniques

Proper assembly ensures your joints reach their full potential:

1. *Dry Fitting*
Essential steps:
- Test all joints before glue
- Check for square
- Mark assembly sequence
- Prepare clamps

Verification process:
- Check joint tightness
- Measure diagonals
- Test alignment
- Review aesthetics

2. *Glue-Up Process*
Organized approach:
- Arrange parts logically

- Apply glue evenly
- Work within open time
- Clean squeeze-out promptly

Special Considerations for Different Woods
Different wood types require different approaches:

Hardwood vs. Softwood

1. *Hardwood Joinery*
Special considerations:
- Tighter tolerances possible
- Stronger glue bonds
- More precise cutting required
- Better screw holding

Technique adjustments:
- Use sharp tools
- Take lighter cuts
- Allow for density
- Consider grain structure

2. *Softwood Joinery*
Working characteristics:
- More forgiving fit
- Faster cutting
- Different glue absorption
- Different screw requirements

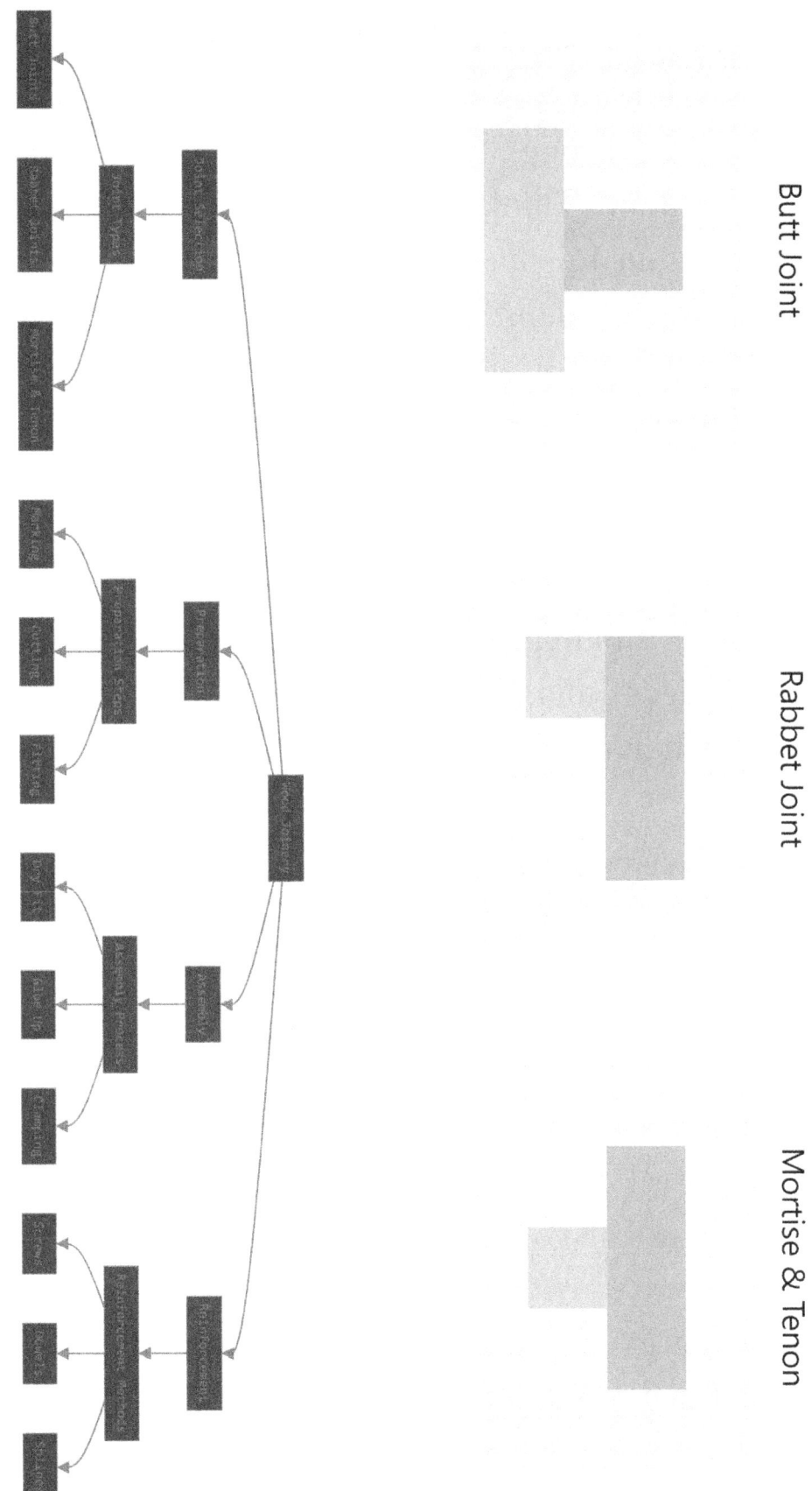

Butt Joint

Rabbet Joint

Mortise & Tenon

193

Sanding and Surface Preparation

Let me guide you through the critical process of sanding and surface preparation. Think of sanding as creating a smooth foundation for your finish – much like how an artist prepares their canvas before painting. The quality of your surface preparation will directly influence the beauty and durability of your final piece.

Understanding Surface Preparation Fundamentals

Before we begin sanding, we need to understand what we're trying to achieve and how wood responds to different preparation techniques.

Initial Surface Assessment

Think of this step as creating a roadmap for your sanding process:

1. *Visual Inspection*
   Systematic check for:
   - Machine marks or gouges
   - Grain tear-out
   - Glue residue
   - Previous finish remnants

194

Process:
- Use raking light to highlight defects
- Mark problem areas with pencil
- Note grain direction changes
- Identify areas needing special attention

2. *Tactile Assessment*
Feel the surface to identify:
- High spots
- Low areas
- Grain raising
- Surface inconsistencies

The Sanding Progression

Proper sanding requires moving through grits in a logical sequence. Think of it as refining the surface in stages, where each grit removes the scratches left by the previous one.

Coarse Grit Phase (60-80 grit)

1. *Initial Leveling*
Process steps:
- Start with clean sandpaper
- Apply even pressure
- Work in systematic pattern
- Check progress frequently

Technique:
- Sand with grain direction
- Use consistent stroke length
- Avoid excessive pressure
- Keep sandpaper clean

2. *Defect Removal*
Addressing problems:
- Level machine marks
- Remove deep scratches
- Eliminate tear-out
- Smooth joints

Medium Grit Phase (120-150 grit)

1. *Surface Refinement*
Key steps:
- Remove coarse grit scratches
- Even out surface texture
- Begin smoothing process
- Prepare for fine sanding

Method:
- Change sanding direction slightly
- Maintain consistent pressure
- Check progress with raking light
- Clean surface between grits

Fine Grit Phase (220+ grit)

1. *Final Smoothing*
Process:
- Remove all previous scratches
- Achieve uniform surface
- Prepare for finishing
- Final inspection

Technique:
- Light, even pressure
- Regular paper cleaning
- Frequent surface checking
- Dust removal between grits

Special Considerations for Different Woods

Different wood types require different approaches:

Hardwoods

1. *Dense Woods*
Special techniques:
- Use fresh sandpaper more frequently
- Progress through grits more gradually
- Watch for burnishing
- Consider grain direction carefully

2. *Open-Grain Woods*
Preparation methods:
- Consider grain filling
- Use proper grit sequence
- Watch for dust in pores
- Clean thoroughly between grits

Softwoods

1. *Resinous Woods*
Special considerations:
- Clean paper frequently
- Watch for heat buildup
- Consider hand sanding
- Use proper paper type

2. *Soft Grain Woods*
Techniques:
- Use light pressure
- Support backing material
- Watch for grain crushing
- Consider sanding sealer

Final Surface Preparation

Preparing for finishing requires attention to detail:

Clean-Up Process

1. *Dust Removal*
Complete process:
- Vacuum surface thoroughly
- Wipe with tack cloth
- Use compressed air if available
- Final inspection

Verification:
- Check corners and edges
- Inspect pores and grain
- Verify surface cleanliness
- Test with white cloth

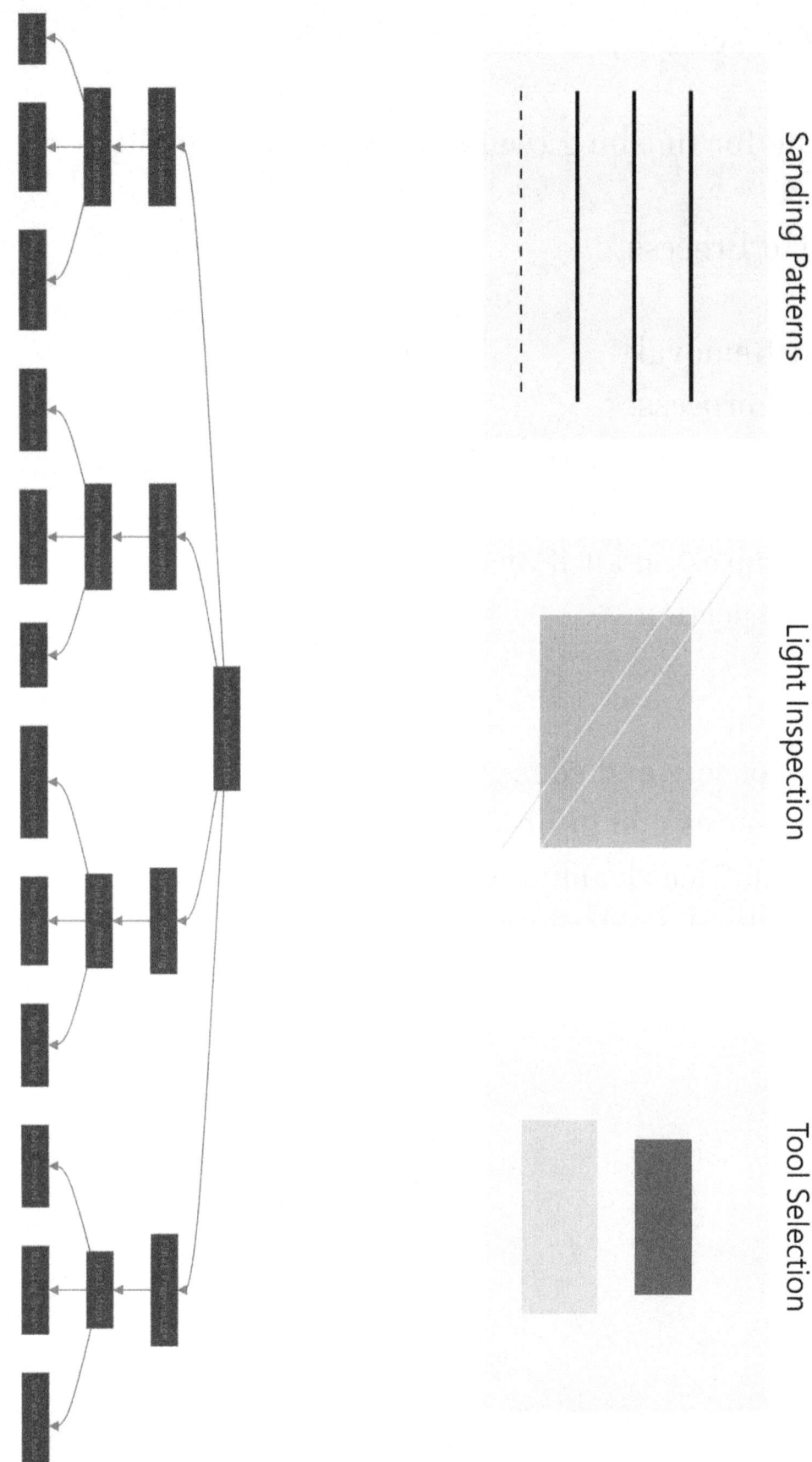

Understanding and Using Wood Glue

Think of wood glue as the invisible foundation that holds your woodworking projects together. Just as a building needs a proper foundation, understanding how wood glue works and how to use it correctly is fundamental to creating lasting joints. Let me walk you through everything you need to know about selecting and using wood glue effectively.

Understanding Wood Glue Types

Different glues serve different purposes, much like how different tools are suited for specific tasks. Let's explore the main types and their applications:

PVA (Polyvinyl Acetate) Glue
The most common type for woodworking:

1. *Yellow Wood Glue (Aliphatic Resin)*
   Characteristics:
   - Stronger than wood when properly used
   - Water-resistant but not waterproof
   - 5-10 minute open time
   - Dries to slight yellow color

   Best uses:
   - Indoor furniture

- General woodworking
- Panel glue-ups
- Basic joinery

2. *White PVA Glue*
Properties:
- Longer open time
- Easier cleanup
- Less water resistant
- Dries clear

Ideal for:
- Craft projects
- Light-duty work
- Interior projects
- When clear glue line desired

Surface Preparation for Gluing

The success of any glue joint begins with proper surface preparation, much like painting requires a clean, properly prepared surface:

Preparing Wood Surfaces

1. *Cleanliness Requirements*
Process steps:
- Remove all dust and debris

- Check for oils or finishes
- Clean with appropriate solvent if needed
- Allow surface to dry completely

Verification methods:
- Visual inspection
- Wipe test with white cloth
- Check for contamination
- Test water absorption

2. *Environmental Conditions*
Critical factors:
- Temperature (65-75°F ideal)
- Humidity (40-60% RH)
- Wood moisture content (6-8%)
- Room temperature

Proper Glue Application

Think of glue application as painting – coverage and technique matter:

Application Methods

1. *Even Coverage*
Technique:
- Apply in consistent pattern
- Use appropriate amount

- Spread evenly
- Watch for dry spots

Common mistakes to avoid:
- Too much glue
- Too little glue
- Uneven application
- Missing spots

2. *Assembly Time Management*
Working within open time:
- Plan assembly sequence
- Have clamps ready
- Work efficiently
- Monitor glue tackiness

Clamping Techniques

Proper clamping is as important as the glue itself:

Basic Clamping Principles

1. *Pressure Requirements*
Guidelines:
- Softwoods: 100-150 psi
- Hardwoods: 150-250 psi
- Edge joints: 100-150 psi
- Face gluing: 150-200 psi

Application method:
- Use enough clamps
- Space evenly
- Check alignment
- Monitor pressure

2. *Clamping Duration*
Timing considerations:
- Minimum 30 minutes for handling
- 24 hours for full strength
- Longer in cold conditions
- Check manufacturer's recommendations

Clean-up and Post-Gluing Care

Proper clean-up affects both appearance and joint strength:

Clean-up Methods

1. *Immediate Clean-up*
Process:
- Remove excess while wet
- Use damp cloth
- Clean corners thoroughly
- Check for drips

Tools needed:
- Clean water
- Clean rags
- Scraper
- Chisel for dried glue

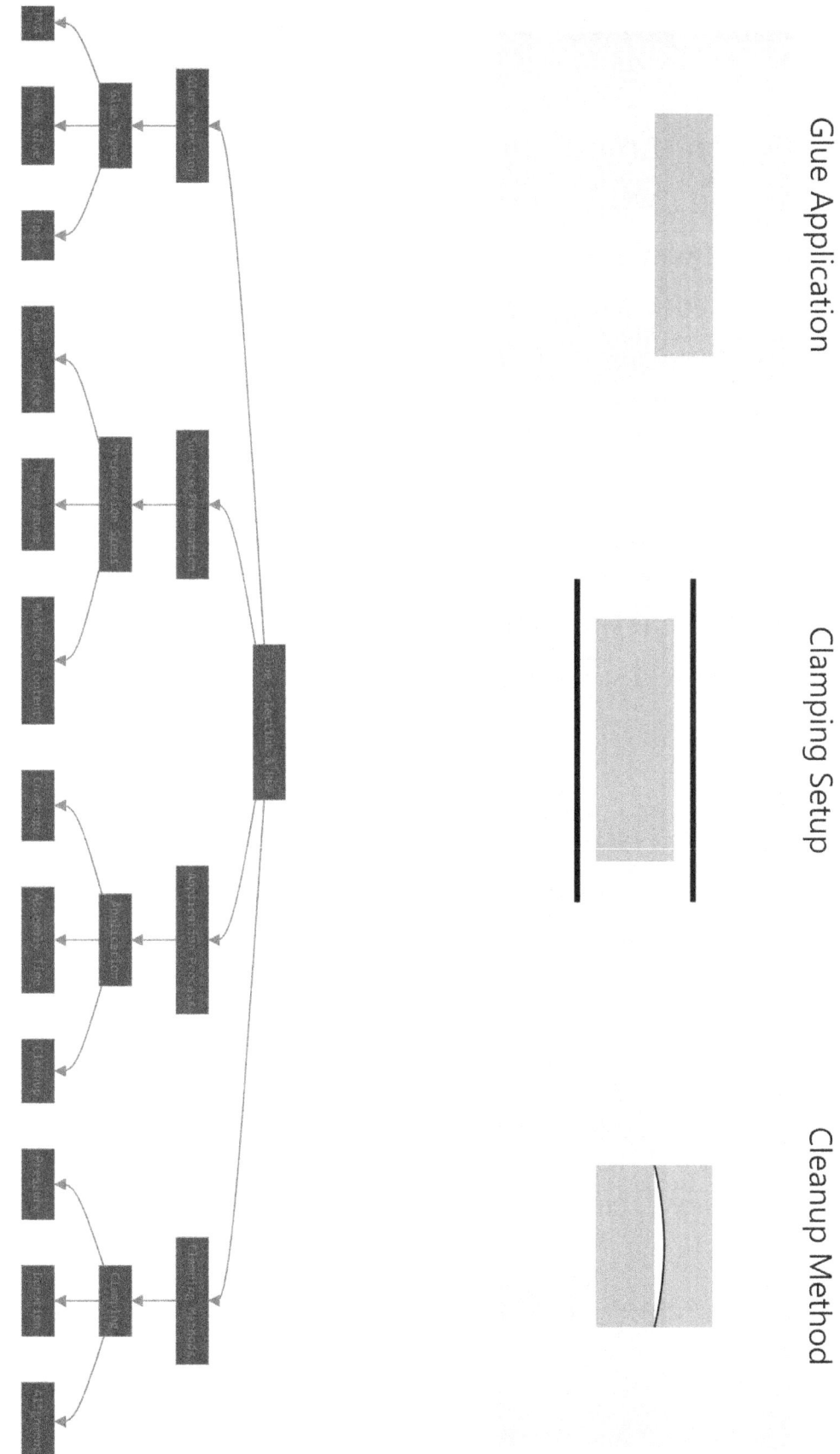

Glue Application

Clamping Setup

Cleanup Method

Basic Joinery for Beginners

Let me guide you through the fundamentals of woodworking joinery, starting with the most basic connections and building up to more complex joints. Think of joinery as the vocabulary of woodworking – starting with simple words and gradually building to more complex sentences.

Understanding Basic Joint Types

Let's begin with the three fundamental joints that every beginner should master. These form the foundation for all woodworking projects:

The Butt Joint

This is the simplest joint, but mastering it teaches crucial lessons about wood alignment and grain direction:

1. *Creating a Basic Butt Joint*
   Process steps:
   - Square both joining surfaces perfectly
   - Mark reference faces clearly
   - Check for tight fit
   - Plan reinforcement method

Implementation:

1. Prepare the surfaces:
- Plane or sand edges square
- Check with try square
- Mark mating surfaces
- Clean thoroughly

2. Test the fit:
- Hold pieces together
- Look for gaps
- Check squareness
- Mark any high spots

The Rabbet Joint

A step up from the butt joint, adding mechanical strength:

1. *Layout Process*
Careful marking is essential:
- Determine rabbet width (typically 1/3 to 1/2 material thickness)
- Mark depth clearly
- Use marking gauge for consistency
- Double-check all measurements

2. *Cutting the Rabbet*
Method options:
a. Using hand tools:
- Score boundaries with knife
- Chisel to depth line
- Clean with router plane
- Test fit frequently

b. Using power tools:
- Set up table saw or router
- Make test cuts
- Cut in multiple passes
- Clean up if needed

The Dado Joint

A strong joint for shelving and case construction:

1. *Layout and Marking*
Precise layout ensures success:
- Mark dado location
- Set dado width
- Establish depth
- Mark waste area

Tools needed:
- Marking gauge
- Square

- Sharp pencil
- Marking knife

2. *Cutting Process*

Step-by-step approach:
- Score boundaries
- Remove waste in stages
- Maintain consistent depth
- Test fit frequently

Essential Joint Layout Skills

Accurate layout is crucial for successful joinery:

Basic Layout Tools

1. *Measuring and Marking Tools*

Essential items:
- Accurate square
- Marking gauge
- Sharp pencil
- Marking knife

Usage techniques:
- Hold tools firmly
- Mark with light pressure
- Use consistent reference faces
- Double-check measurements

2. *Layout Process*
Systematic approach:
- Start from reference edge
- Mark baseline first
- Transfer measurements carefully
- Review before cutting

Joint Cutting Techniques

Proper cutting ensures strong joints:

Hand Tool Methods

1. *Using Chisels*
Basic technique:
- Start with sharp tools
- Work from layout lines
- Take controlled cuts
- Check progress frequently

Key points:
- Keep tools sharp
- Use appropriate size
- Work systematically
- Test fit often

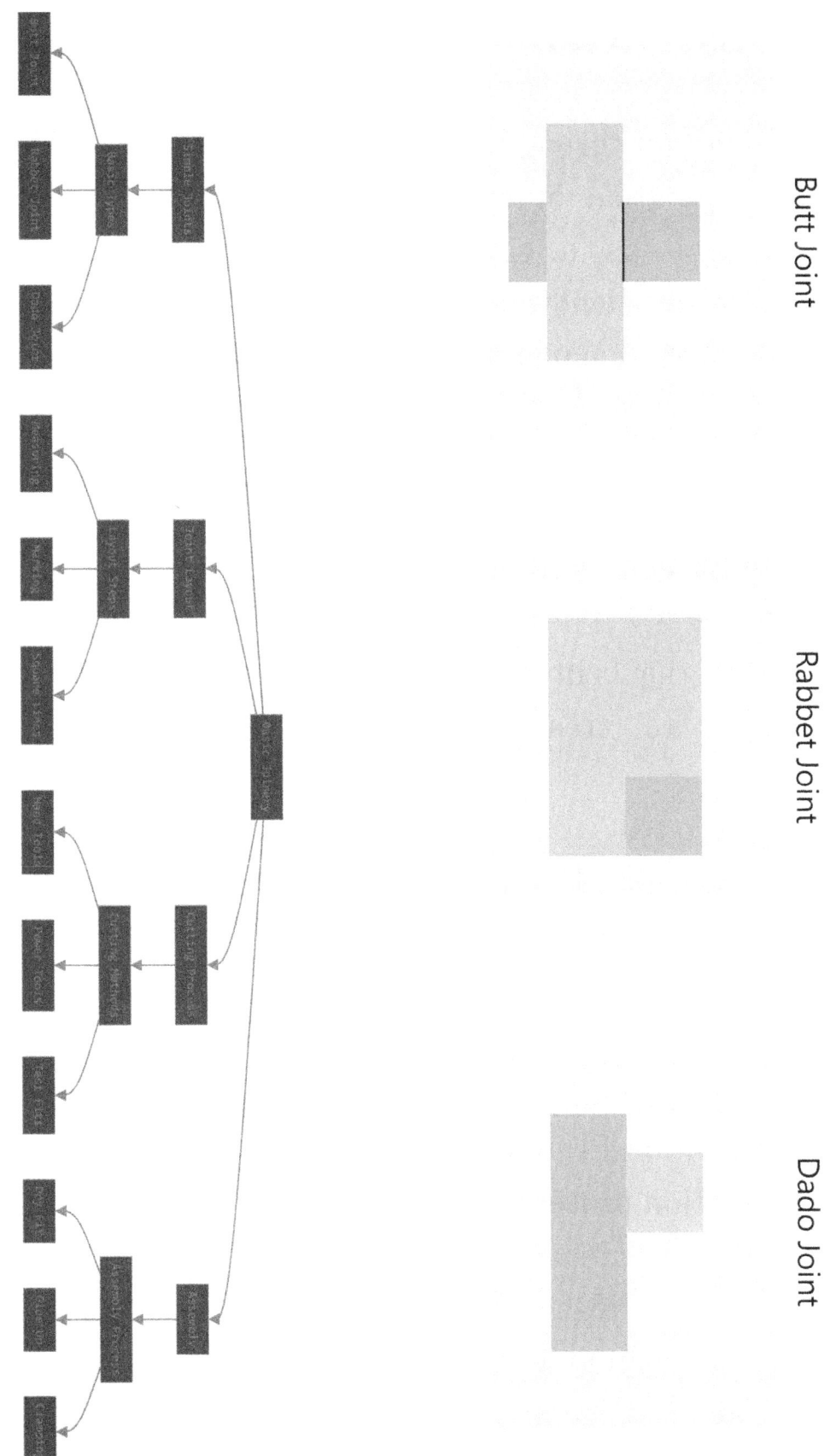

Butt Joint

Rabbet Joint

Dado Joint

213

Essential Workshop Skills

Let me guide you through the essential workshop skills that form the foundation of successful woodworking. Think of your workshop as a carefully orchestrated environment where safety, efficiency, and organization work together to enable your craftsmanship. I'll break down these crucial skills into manageable components and explain how they interconnect.

Workshop Safety Fundamentals

Safety forms the bedrock of all workshop activities. Let's explore how to create and maintain a safe working environment:

Personal Protection Equipment (PPE)

Think of PPE as your armor in the workshop. Here's how to develop proper PPE habits:

1. *Eye Protection Protocol*
   Implementation process:
   - Select appropriate safety glasses
   - Ensure proper fit
   - Keep them clean and accessible
   - Wear them consistently

Key considerations:
- Consider side protection
- Use face shield when needed
- Keep spare pairs handy
- Replace damaged equipment

2. *Hearing Protection*
Usage guidelines:
- Choose appropriate type
- Understand noise levels
- Maintain clean condition
- Monitor effectiveness

Tool Management and Care

Proper tool management extends tool life and ensures safety:

Tool Organization Systems

Think of tool organization as creating a map where everything has its place:

1. *Wall Storage Implementation*
Process steps:
- Analyze tool frequency of use
- Design logical groupings
- Install appropriate holders
- Label clearly

Organization method:
- Frequently used tools at easy reach
- Similar tools together
- Clear visibility
- Easy access and return

2. *Bench Organization*
Setup process:
- Create zones for different tasks
- Establish tool parking spots
- Maintain clear work area
- Plan for project needs

Tool Maintenance

Regular maintenance preserves tool function and safety:

1. *Daily Maintenance*
Routine tasks:
- Clean after use
- Check for damage
- Oil moving parts
- Store properly

Implementation:
- Create checklist
- Set maintenance schedule
- Document issues

- Track repairs

Work Organization and Efficiency

Efficient work habits multiply your effectiveness:

Workflow Planning

Think of workflow as choreographing a dance:

1. *Project Setup*
Organization process:
- Plan material storage
- Arrange tools needed
- Set up work supports
- Establish assembly area

Considerations:
- Material movement
- Tool accessibility
- Light and space
- Power tool placement

2. *Process Sequencing*
Planning steps:
- List operations needed
- Order tasks logically
- Plan material handling

- Allow for drying time

Problem-Solving Skills

Developing systematic problem-solving approaches:

Troubleshooting Process

1. *Problem Assessment*
Systematic approach:
- Identify symptoms
- Gather information
- Consider causes
- Document findings

Implementation:
- Use all senses
- Take detailed notes
- Research similar issues
- Consult resources

2. *Solution Development*
Process steps:
- List possible solutions
- Evaluate options
- Test solutions
- Document results

Workshop Environment

Creating an effective working environment:

Climate Control

1. *Temperature Management*
Considerations:
- Maintain consistent temperature
- Control humidity
- Provide ventilation
- Monitor conditions

Implementation:
- Install thermometer
- Use dehumidifier if needed
- Ensure air circulation
- Check regularly

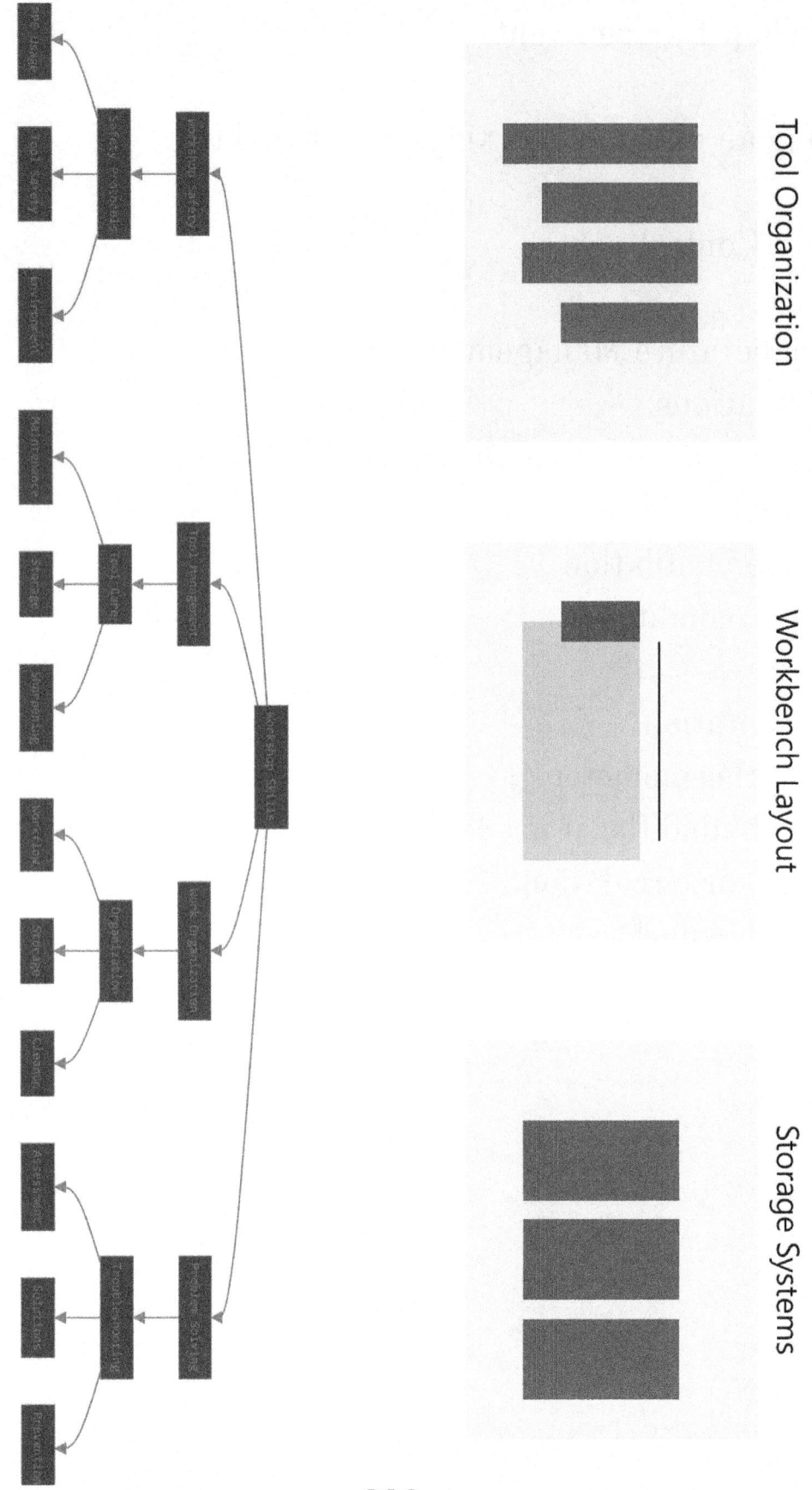

Tool Organization

Workbench Layout

Storage Systems

220

Chapter 6
Project Planning and Execution

Organizing Your Workflow

Let me guide you through the essential process of organizing your woodworking workflow. Think of workflow organization as composing a symphony where every element has its proper time and place, working together to create a harmonious whole. A well-organized workflow not only makes your work more efficient but also helps prevent mistakes and ensures consistent quality.

Project Planning Phase

The foundation of successful workflow organization begins with thorough planning. Let's break this down into manageable components:

Initial Project Analysis

Think of this as creating a detailed map for your journey:

1. *Project Documentation Development*
   Start by creating a comprehensive project file:

- Detailed drawings with dimensions
- Materials list with specifications
- Tool requirements
- Timeline estimates

Implementation process:
- Create digital or paper folder
- Include all reference materials
- Make detailed notes
- Add sketches and photos

2. *Resource Assessment*
Evaluate everything you'll need:
- Material requirements
- Tool availability
- Space needs
- Time constraints

Timeline Development

Creating a realistic timeline is crucial for project success:

1. *Task Breakdown*
Process steps:
- List all required tasks
- Estimate time for each
- Identify dependencies
- Build in buffer time

Organization method:
- Use spreadsheet or project software
- Create visual timeline
- Mark critical paths
- Note deadlines

Workspace Organization

An efficient workspace layout is essential for smooth workflow:

Work Zones Setup

Think of your workspace as a series of connected stations:

1. *Zone Definition*
Create distinct areas for:
- Material storage and preparation
- Machine work
- Assembly
- Finishing
- Tool storage

Implementation:
- Map out zones on paper first
- Consider material flow
- Optimize walking paths
- Plan for power needs

2. *Zone Organization*
Within each zone:
- Arrange tools logically
- Provide adequate lighting
- Ensure proper ventilation
- Include cleanup stations

Process Management

Managing the actual workflow requires attention to detail:

Daily Planning

1. *Task Prioritization*
Start each day by:
- Reviewing project timeline
- Setting daily goals
- Organizing materials
- Preparing tools

Implementation:
- Use checklist system
- Track progress
- Adjust as needed
- Document changes

2. *Workflow Sequence*
Maintain efficient process flow:
- Complete similar tasks together
- Minimize tool changes
- Optimize material handling
- Plan for natural breaks

Quality Control Integration

Build quality checks into your workflow:

Checkpoint System

1. *Critical Checkpoints*
Establish verification points:
- After material preparation
- Before assembly
- After major steps
- Before finishing

Implementation:
- Create checkpoint checklist
- Document inspections
- Address issues immediately
- Track recurring problems

2. *Documentation Process*
Record keeping for quality:
- Take progress photos
- Note measurements
- Document changes
- Keep material records

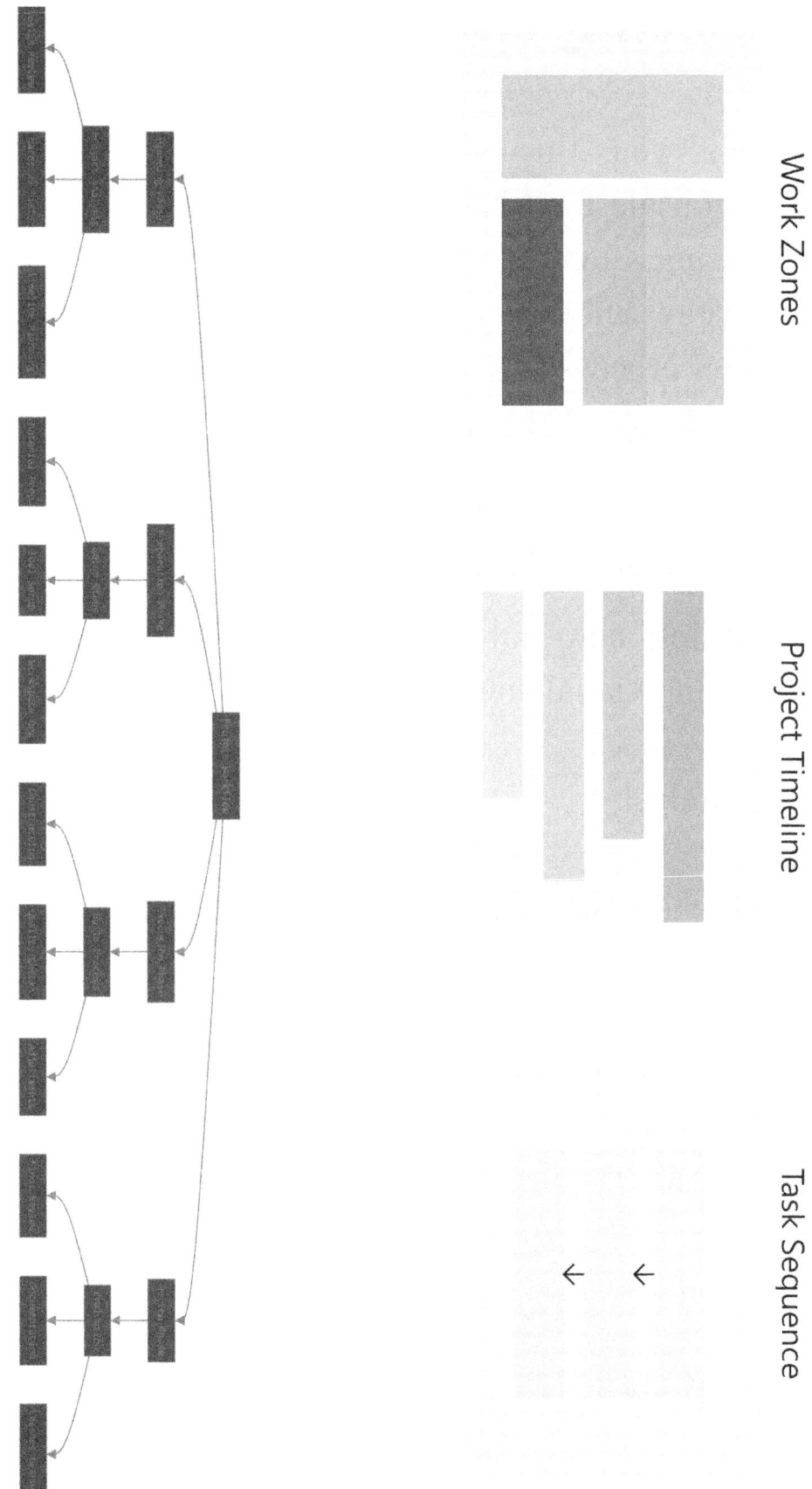

Work Zones

Project Timeline

Task Sequence

Calculating Materials Needed

Let me guide you through the systematic process of calculating materials for your woodworking projects. Think of this as creating a detailed shopping list that not only tells you what to buy but also helps you use those materials efficiently. This process is crucial for both cost management and project success.

Creating a Detailed Parts List

Before calculating materials, we need to break down the project into its individual components:

Component Analysis

1. *Primary Parts List*
   Start by listing every piece needed:
   - Identify each component
   - Note finished dimensions
   - Specify wood type
   - Document grain requirements

   Process example:
   ```

   Component: Table Top
   - Finished size: 36" x 72" x 1.5"
   - Material: White Oak
   ```

- Grain: Long grain running length
- Boards needed: 6 pieces @ 6" width
```


2. *Secondary Components*
Don't forget supporting pieces:
- Drawer parts
- Interior components
- Support pieces
- Test pieces


## Material Calculations

Now let's convert our parts list into actual material requirements:

Rough Lumber Calculations

1. *Board Foot Calculation*
Formula:
```

Board Feet = (Thickness × Width × Length) ÷ 144
```


Implementation steps:
- Add rough cutting allowance
- Include waste factor (20-30%)
- Consider grain matching
```

- Account for defects

2. *Sheet Goods Calculation*
Process for plywood and panels:
- Lay out parts on standard sheet sizes
- Consider grain direction
- Plan efficient cuts
- Include waste factor

Optimization Strategies

Think of optimization as putting together a puzzle:

1. *Cutting Layout Planning*
Steps for efficient material use:
- Draw full-size cutting diagram
- Group similar sized pieces
- Consider grain matching
- Plan cut sequence

Implementation:
- Use graph paper or software
- Label all pieces
- Include kerf allowance
- Note grain direction

2. *Waste Reduction*
Strategies to minimize waste:
- Nest smaller parts in offcuts
- Plan sequential cuts
- Save usable scraps
- Label offcuts for future use

Hardware and Accessories

Don't forget the non-wood components:

Hardware Inventory

1. *Fasteners*
Calculate quantities needed:
- Screws by size and type
- Nails if required
- Special fasteners
- Add 20% extra

Documentation:
```

Screws needed:
- 24 × #8 1-1/4" wood screws
- 16 × #6 3/4" drawer screws
- 8 × 2" pocket hole screws
```

2. *Specialized Hardware*
List all additional items:
- Hinges
- Drawer slides
- Pulls and knobs
- Special mounting hardware

Cost Estimation

Create a detailed budget based on your calculations:

Material Costs

1. *Primary Materials*
Calculate costs for:
- Lumber (by board foot)
- Sheet goods
- Hardware
- Finishing supplies

Documentation format:
```

White Oak @ $8.50/bf × 45 bf = $382.50
3/4" Plywood @ $65/sheet × 2 = $130
Hardware package = $85
Finish supplies = $45
```

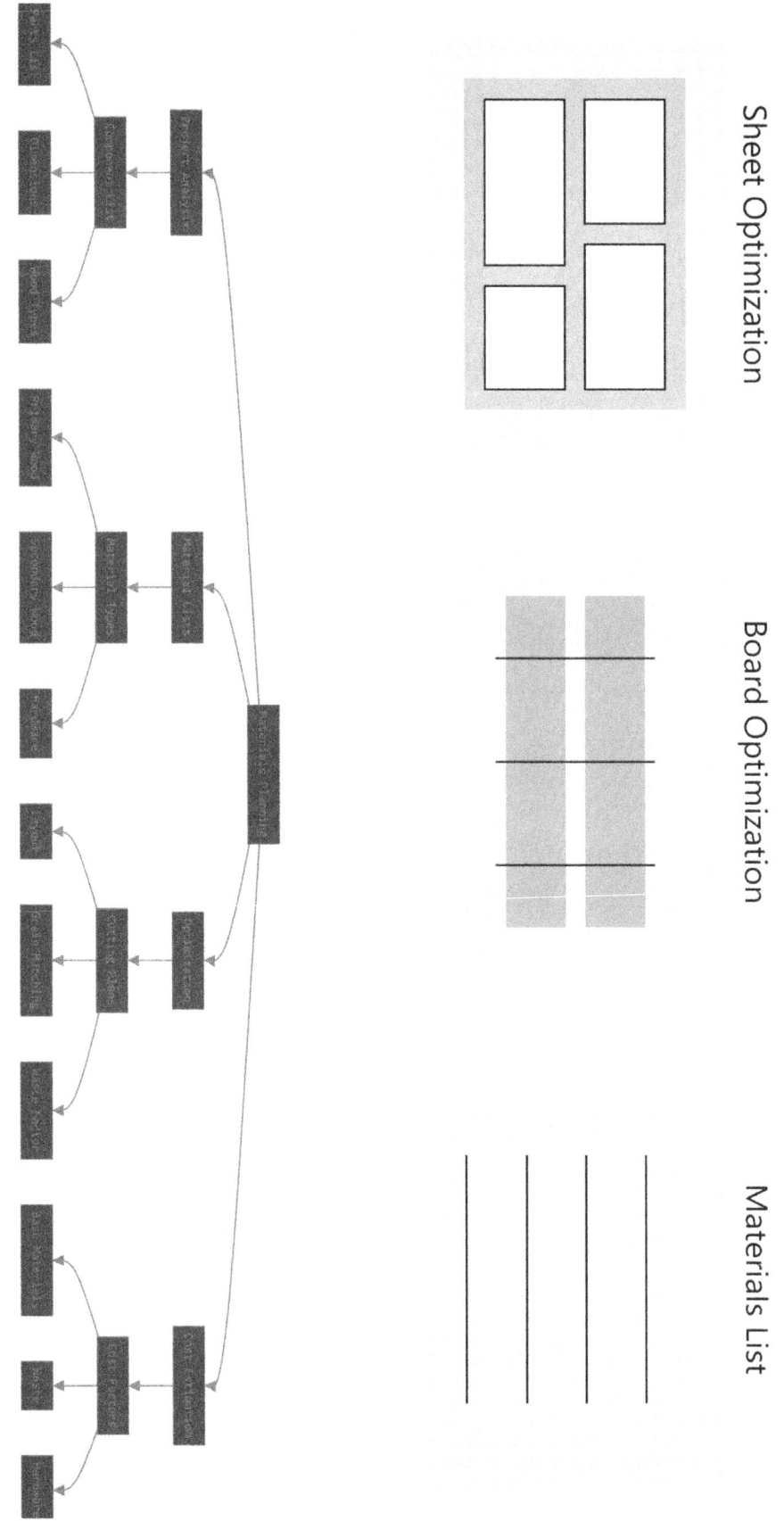

Sheet Optimization

Board Optimization

Materials List

233

Making a Cut List

Let me guide you through the process of creating an effective cut list, a crucial planning tool that serves as your project's roadmap. Think of a cut list as a detailed recipe for your woodworking project – it tells you exactly what pieces you need, their sizes, and how they fit together.

Understanding Cut List Fundamentals

Before we dive into creating a cut list, let's understand its core components and purpose. A well-organized cut list not only helps you work efficiently but also reduces waste and prevents costly mistakes.

Basic Cut List Structure

A comprehensive cut list should include several key elements:

1. *Essential Information Fields*
   For each part, record:
   - Part name/description
   - Quantity needed
   - Final dimensions (length $\times$ width $\times$ thickness)
   - Material type
   - Grain direction requirements
   - Special notes

Example format:
```

Part: Table Top
Qty: 1
Size: 36"L × 24"W × 1.75"T
Material: White Oak
Grain: Length
Notes: Book-matched panels
```


Creating an Organized Cut List

Let's break down the process of creating a detailed cut list:

Phase 1: Project Analysis

Start by analyzing your project drawings:

1. *Component Identification*
Process steps:
- Review all project drawings
- List every unique part
- Note quantities needed
- Identify similar parts

Documentation approach:
- Use consistent naming
- Group related parts

- Number or code each part
- Include reference sketches

Phase 2: Dimensional Planning

Account for all sizing requirements:

1. *Size Calculations*
Include allowances for:
- Final dimensions
- Rough cutting
- Joinery
- Sanding/finishing

Calculation example:
```

Final size: 24" length
+ 1/4" joinery allowance
+ 1" rough cutting allowance
= 25-1/4" rough length needed
```

Phase 3: Material Organization

Group parts by material type and cutting sequence:

1. *Material Categories*
Organize by:

- Primary wood species
- Secondary woods
- Sheet goods
- Thickness requirements

Implementation:
- Create separate sections
- Note stock requirements
- Consider grain matching
- Plan efficient use

2. *Cutting Sequence*
Plan your workflow:
- Start with longest parts
- Group similar lengths
- Consider tool setup
- Minimize waste

Documentation and Reference

Create clear, usable documentation:

Cut List Format

1. *Layout Design*
Include columns for:
- Part number/name
- Quantity

- Dimensions
- Material
- Notes
- Status/completion

Format example:
```

# | Part Name | Qty | L × W × T | Material | Notes
1 | Top | 1 | 36×24×1.75| Oak | Grain→length
2 | Legs | 4 | 29×3×3 | Oak | Quarter-sawn
```


2. *Additional Information*
Include supporting details:
- Project name and date
- Material specifications
- Special instructions
- Reference drawings

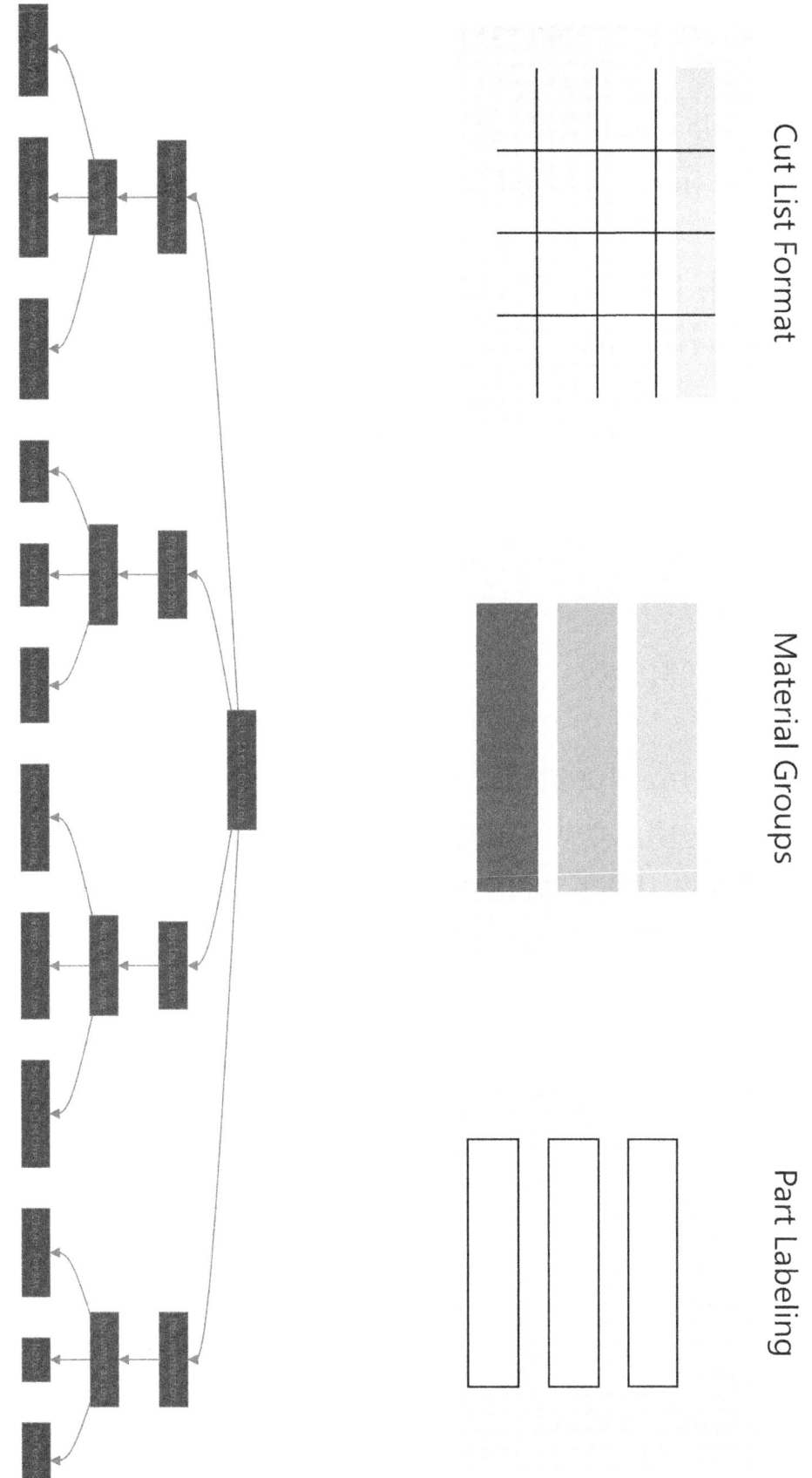

Cut List Format

Material Groups

Part Labeling

239

Time Management in Woodworking

Let me guide you through the essential aspects of time management in woodworking. Think of time management as the invisible framework that supports every successful project, much like how a well-designed jig guides your tools to create precise cuts. By mastering time management, you'll not only complete projects more efficiently but also enjoy the process more thoroughly.

Understanding Project Time Management

First, let's explore how to develop a comprehensive understanding of project time requirements. Time management in woodworking is unique because it must account for both predictable processes and variable factors like glue drying times or finish curing.

Project Timeline Development

Just as you wouldn't start cutting wood without measuring, you shouldn't start a project without a timeline. Here's how to create one effectively:

1. *Project Phase Identification*
   Think of your project in distinct phases:
   - Material preparation
   - Component creation

- Assembly
- Finishing

For each phase, consider:
``` `

Phase: Material Preparation
Tasks:
- Stock selection (1 hour)
- Rough cutting (2 hours)
- Milling to size (3 hours)
- Acclimation time (48 hours)
``` `

2. *Realistic Time Allocation*
For each task, consider:
- Setup time
- Active work time
- Cleanup time
- Buffer for unexpected issues

Task Organization and Sequencing

Efficient task organization is like creating a well-organized tool cabinet – everything has its place and purpose.

Creating Task Sequences

1. *Logical Task Grouping*
Organize tasks by:
- Tool setup requirements
- Material types
- Process similarities
- Location in workshop

Implementation example:
```

Morning Session:
1. All table saw cuts (minimize setup changes)
2. Router work (while dust collection is set up)
3. Assembly prep (transition to clean work)
```

2. *Dependency Management*
Track task relationships:
- What must be completed first?
- What can be done simultaneously?
- What requires waiting periods?
- What affects multiple components?

Time Optimization Techniques

Think of time optimization as finding the most efficient path through your workshop:

Setup Time Reduction

1. *Tool Organization*
Implement systematic organization:
- Keep frequently used tools accessible
- Create dedicated tool stations
- Maintain sharp tools ready for use
- Organize consumables efficiently

Example setup:
```

Primary Workbench Zone:
- Measuring tools within arm's reach
- Power tools on lower shelf
- Jigs organized by type
- Safety equipment at entry point
```

2. *Batch Processing*
Group similar operations:
- Cut all similar parts together
- Do all routing with same bit
- Sand all pieces of same grit
- Apply finish to multiple pieces

Progress Tracking and Adjustment

Just as you measure twice and cut once, regular progress assessment ensures you stay on track:

Documentation System

1. *Daily Progress Log*
Record key information:
- Tasks completed
- Time spent
- Challenges encountered
- Solutions found

Format example:
```

Date: [Today's Date]
Completed: Table legs shaping
Time: 3.5 hours
Notes: Grain tear-out on leg #3 - adjusted technique
Tomorrow: Complete leg sanding, begin aprons
```

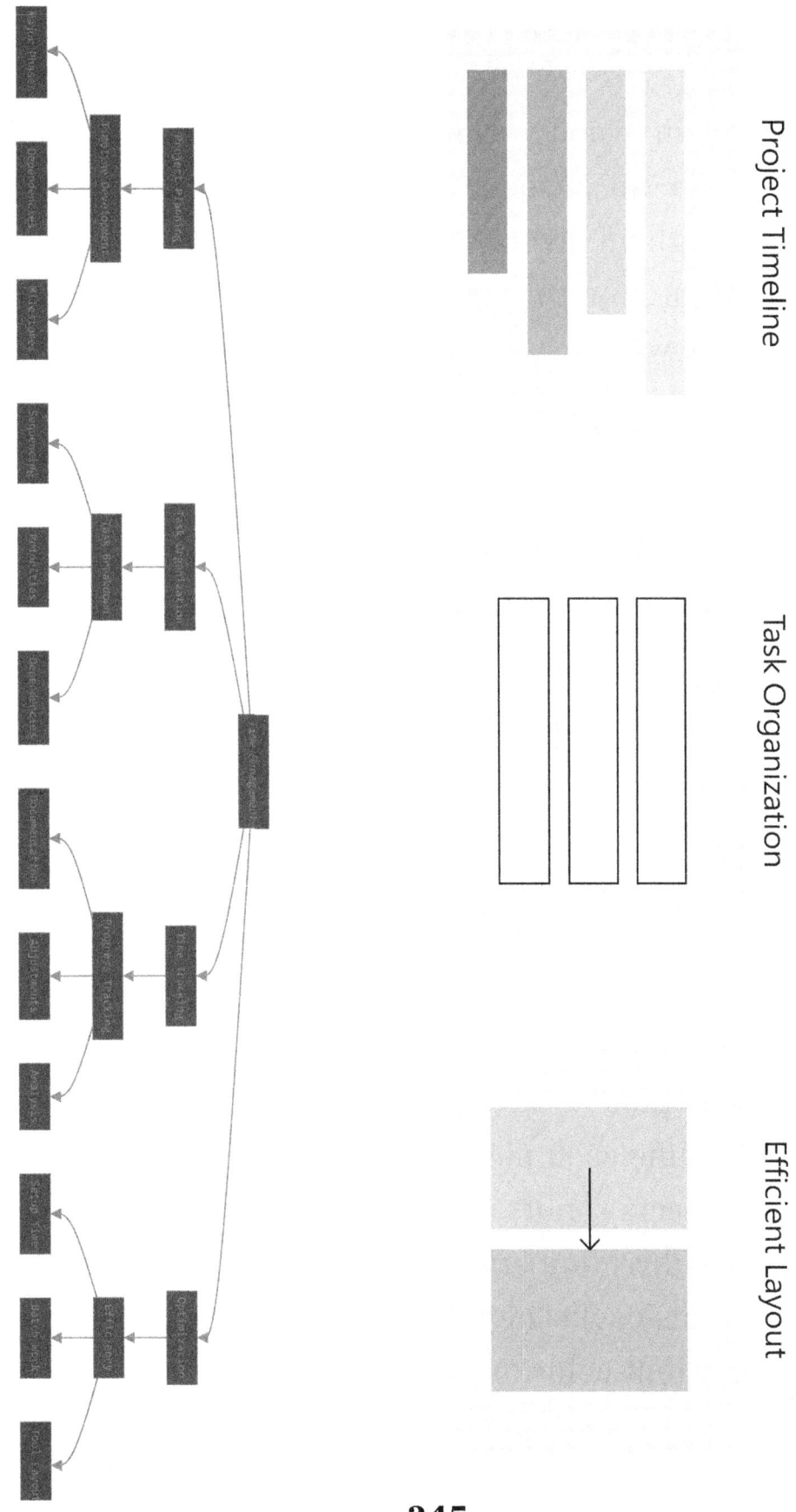

Project Timeline

Task Organization

Efficient Layout

Quality Control Checkpoints

Quality control in woodworking is much like being both a craftsperson and an inspector - you must maintain high standards throughout every stage of your project. Let me walk you through how to implement effective quality control checkpoints that will ensure excellence in your woodworking projects.

Initial Material Assessment

Just as a chef inspects ingredients before cooking, your first quality control checkpoint begins before you make your first cut. Think of this as establishing your project's foundation.

Material Inspection Process

When examining your materials, follow this systematic approach:

1. *Visual Inspection*
   Carefully examine each piece of wood:
   - Check for defects (knots, splits, checks)
   - Assess grain direction and pattern
   - Look for stains or discoloration
   - Verify consistent color matching

Documentation example:
```

Material: White Oak Board #1
Grade: FAS
Defects: Small knot at 24" from end
Grain: Straight, consistent
Color: Matches sample board
Action: Mark knot for cutting around
```


2. *Moisture Content Verification*
Test and record moisture levels:
- Use moisture meter in multiple locations
- Document readings
- Compare to desired range
- Note any variations

Process Quality Control

Think of process quality control as creating checkpoints along your journey. These are the moments where you stop to verify everything is proceeding as planned.

Dimensional Accuracy

1. *Measurement Protocols*
Implement systematic checking:
- Measure at multiple points

- Use consistent reference faces
- Document measurements
- Compare to plans

Measurement log format:
```

Component: Table Leg #1
Required: 29" × 3" × 3"
Actual: 29-1/16" × 3-1/32" × 3"
Tolerance: Within ±1/32"
Status: Acceptable
```

2. *Squareness and Alignment*
Check critical angles:
- Use reliable square
- Verify multiple faces
- Test assembled components
- Document results

Assembly Quality Control

As components come together, new quality checkpoints become crucial:

Joint Fitting

1. *Dry Assembly Checks*
 Before glue-up:
 - Test fit all joints
 - Check alignments
 - Verify gaps
 - Test functionality

Joint assessment criteria:
```

Joint Type: Mortise and Tenon
Fit: Snug but not tight
Gap Tolerance: <0.005"
Alignment: Square to reference
Action: Approved for glue-up
```


Final Quality Review

Think of this as your project's final exam:

Comprehensive Inspection

1. *Visual Review*
 Examine overall appearance:
 - Check for consistent gaps
 - Verify surface preparation
 - Assess wood matching
 - Look for any defects

Final checklist:
``` ` ` ` ```

☐ All joints tight and flush
☐ Surfaces ready for finish
☐ Hardware properly fitted
☐ Moving parts function smoothly
☐ No visible defects or damage
``` ` ` ` ```

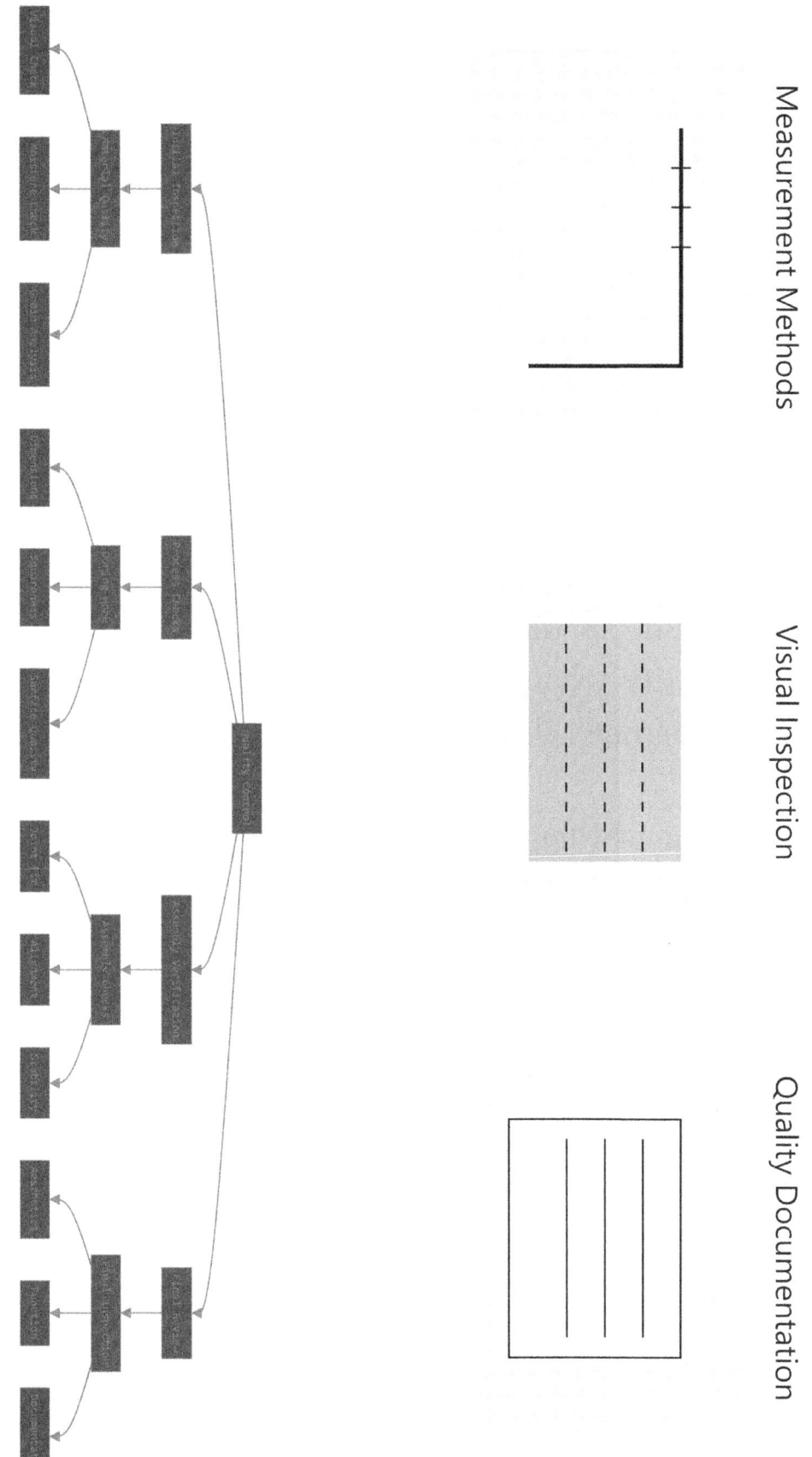

Measurement Methods

Visual Inspection

Quality Documentation

251

Problem-Solving Common Issues

Let me guide you through a systematic approach to identifying, analyzing, and resolving common woodworking problems. Think of this process as being a detective in your workshop - gathering clues, analyzing evidence, and developing solutions that not only fix the immediate issue but prevent future occurrences.

Problem Identification Process

The first step in solving any woodworking problem is to accurately identify what's wrong. Let's break this down into a systematic approach that helps pinpoint issues precisely.

Initial Assessment Phase

When you encounter a problem, follow these steps for thorough evaluation:

1. *Visual Examination*
   Systematically observe the issue:
   - Look at the problem from multiple angles
   - Use good lighting
   - Compare to reference materials
   - Document what you see

Documentation example:
```

Problem Area: Table leg joint
Visual Signs: Gap on inside corner
Size of Issue: 1/32" gap
Pattern: Consistent along length
Additional Notes: No visible damage
```

2. *Physical Testing*
 Carefully test the affected area:
 - Check for movement
 - Test stability
 - Feel for irregularities
 - Note any sounds

Root Cause Analysis

Once you've identified the problem, determining its cause is crucial for proper resolution.

Systematic Analysis Process

1. *Tool-Related Issues*
Check your tools for:
 - Proper setup and alignment
 - Sharp cutting edges
 - Accurate settings

- Calibration status

Analysis checklist:
``` ` ` `

☐ Tool maintenance status
☐ Recent calibration check
☐ Appropriate tool for task
☐ Proper setup verified
☐ Operating condition
` ` `

2. *Material-Related Issues*
Examine material factors:
- Moisture content
- Grain direction
- Material defects
- Storage conditions

Solution Implementation

Developing and implementing solutions requires a methodical approach:

Immediate Solutions

1. *Quick Fixes*
For immediate resolution:
- Identify temporary solutions
```

- Assess impact on final product
- Document fix applied
- Plan for permanent solution

Implementation steps:
```

1. Stop further damage
2. Stabilize affected area
3. Document temporary fix
4. Plan permanent solution
5. Test repair effectiveness
```


2. *Long-term Solutions*
Develop permanent fixes:
- Research proper techniques
- Gather necessary materials
- Plan repair sequence
- Test on scrap first

Prevention Strategies

Think of prevention as vaccination against future problems:

Process Improvement

1. *Workflow Analysis*
Review and improve:

- Tool setup procedures
- Material handling
- Quality checkpoints
- Documentation methods

Implementation plan:
```

Step 1: Document current process
Step 2: Identify weak points
Step 3: Research improvements
Step 4: Test new methods
Step 5: Update procedures
```


2. *Skill Development*
Focus on improvement:
- Practice problem areas
- Learn new techniques
- Seek expert advice
- Document lessons learned

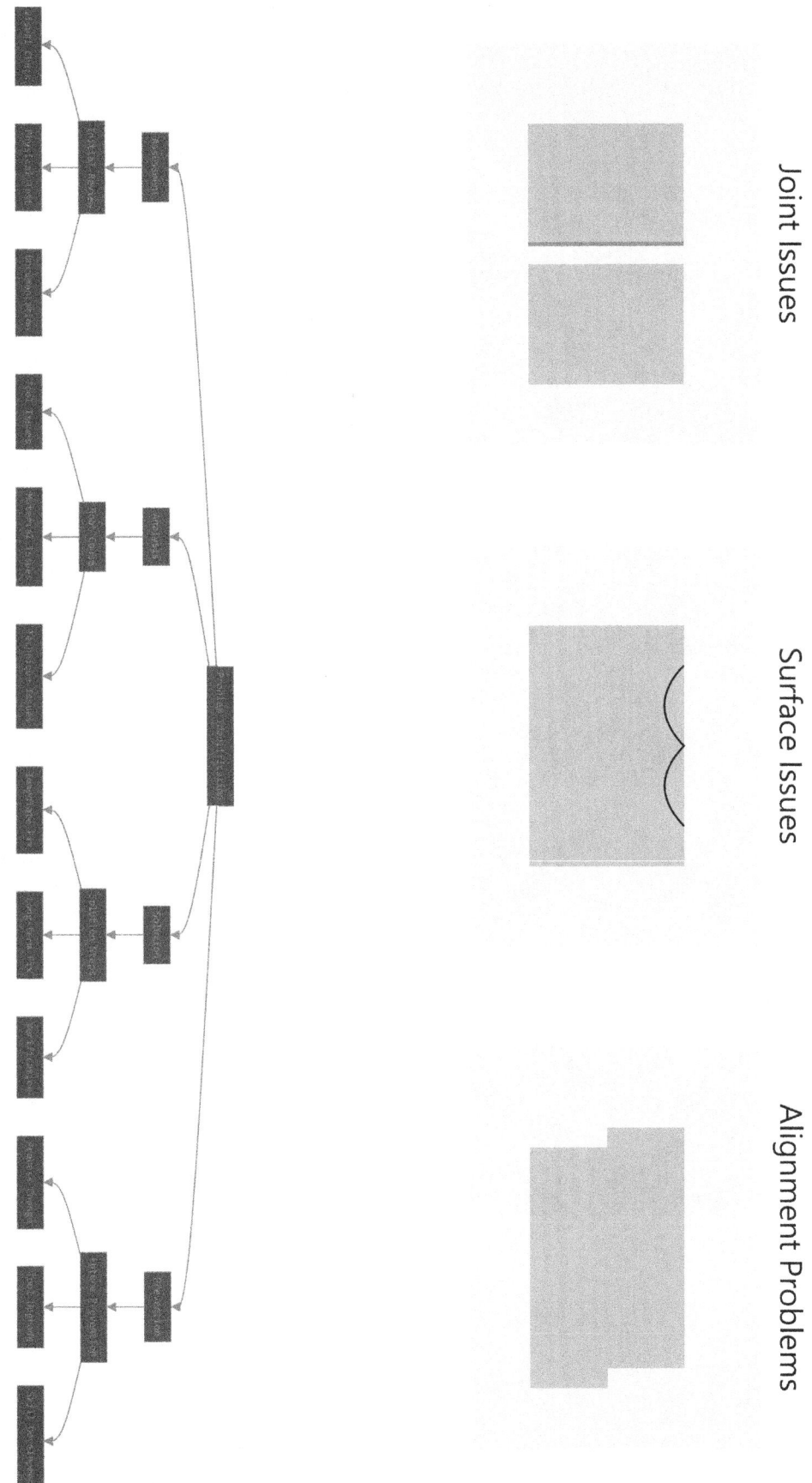

Joint Issues

Surface Issues

Alignment Problems

257

Chapter 7
Finishing Techniques

Understanding Wood Finishes

Let me guide you through understanding wood finishes, starting with the basics and progressing to advanced techniques. Think of wood finish as both a protective shield and an enhancement to the wood's natural beauty.

Understanding Finish Types

Different finishes serve different purposes. Let's explore the main categories and their characteristics:

Oil-Based Finishes

1. *Natural Oils*
   Properties and uses:
   - Penetrating protection
   - Enhanced wood grain
   - Easy maintenance
   - Natural appearance

Application process:
```

1. Sand to 180-grit
```

2. Clean surface thoroughly
3. Apply thin coat
4. Wait 15-20 minutes
5. Wipe excess
6. Allow 24 hours between coats
```


2. *Oil-Based Polyurethane*
Characteristics:
- Durable protection
- Amber color
- Longer dry time
- Chemical resistant

## Water-Based Finishes

Modern alternatives with specific advantages:

1. *Water-Based Polyurethane*
Benefits:
- Quick drying
- Low odor
- Clear finish
- Easy cleanup

Application technique:
```

1. Raise grain and sand

2. Apply thin coats
3. Light sand between coats
4. Multiple thin layers
5. Final buffing
``` `

Application Methods

Different methods suit different finishes and projects:

Brush Application

1. *Brush Selection*
Choose based on:
- Finish type
- Surface size
- Detail requirements
- Project scale

Technique details:
``` `

Stroke Pattern:
1. Load brush properly
2. Start from dry edge
3. Long, even strokes
4. Maintain wet edge
5. Follow grain direction
``` `
```

Wipe-On Application

Perfect for oils and some polyurethanes:

1. *Material Selection*
Choose appropriate applicator:
- Lint-free cloth
- Foam applicator
- Specialty pads
- Clean rags

Process steps:
```

1. Fold applicator properly
2. Saturate but not dripping
3. Apply in circular motion
4. Follow with grain
5. Remove excess promptly
```

Environmental Considerations

Success depends on proper conditions:

Temperature Control

1. *Optimal Conditions*
Maintain:

- 65-75°F temperature
- 40-60% humidity
- Good ventilation
- Dust-free environment

Monitoring system:
```

☐ Temperature gauge
☐ Humidity meter
☐ Air flow check
☐ Dust control measures
```

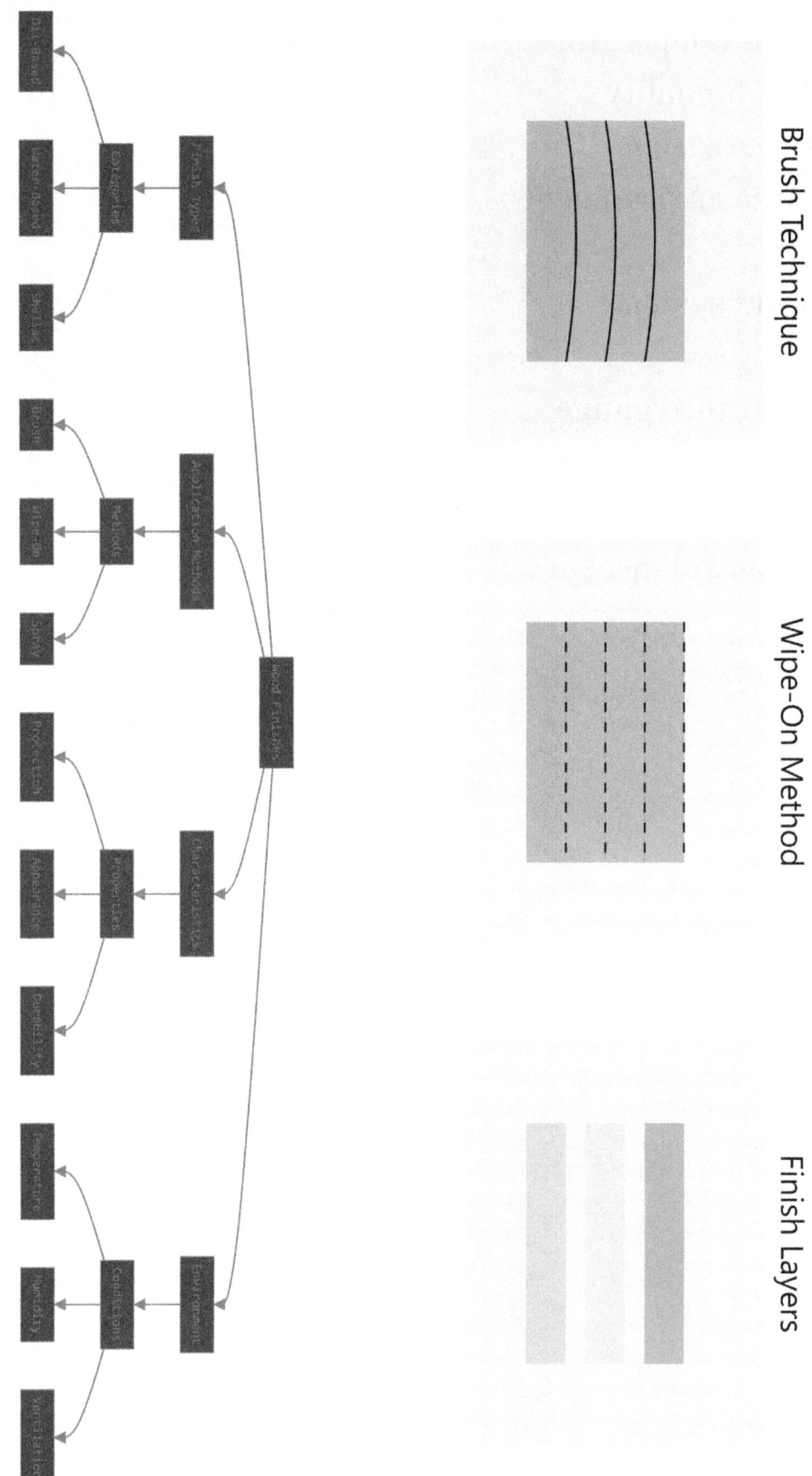

Brush Technique

Wipe-On Method

Finish Layers

264

Surface Preparation

Let me guide you through the critical process of preparing wood surfaces for finishing. Think of surface preparation as building the foundation of a house - the quality of your finish can only be as good as the surface beneath it.

Initial Surface Assessment

Before beginning any preparation work, a thorough assessment is crucial:

Surface Evaluation Process

1. *Visual Inspection*
   Systematic check for:
   - Machine marks
   - Dents and scratches
   - Glue residue
   - Grain tear-out

   Documentation method:
   ```

   Area: Table top
   Issues found:
   - Light planning marks at 12" from edge
   - Minor dent near corner
   - Glue spot from clamp
   ```

Action items listed by priority
```

2. *Physical Inspection*
Tactile examination:
- Feel for rough spots
- Identify raised grain
- Locate high/low spots
- Check edges and corners

**Progressive Sanding Sequence**

Think of sanding as gradually refining the surface, like focusing a camera lens:

Coarse Sanding Phase (60-80 grit)

1. *Initial Leveling*
Process steps:
- Start with clean paper
- Work systematically
- Check progress frequently
- Maintain even pressure

Technique details:
```

1. Sand with grain direction
2. Overlap strokes by 50%

3. Check surface with raking light
4. Mark problem areas
5. Clean surface between grits
``` `

Medium Grit Phase (120-150 grit)

1. *Surface Refinement*
Method:
- Remove previous scratches
- Even out texture
- Check progress regularly
- Clean thoroughly between grits

Procedure:
``` `

1. Change sanding direction slightly
2. Use consistent pressure
3. Check surface frequently
4. Clean dust between grits
5. Verify all coarse scratches removed
``` `
```

Defect Repair Process

Address surface issues systematically:

Dent and Scratch Repair

1. *Steam Treatment for Dents*
Process:
```

1. Dampen dent with water
2. Apply hot iron through cloth
3. Allow wood fibers to swell
4. Let dry completely
5. Sand level if needed
```


2. *Filling Methods*
Options and applications:
- Wood filler for large voids
- Sawdust/glue mix for small gaps
- Epoxy for structural issues
- Color-matched fillers

Final Surface Preparation

The last steps before finishing:

Dust Removal Process

1. *Systematic Cleaning*
Steps:
```

1. Vacuum all surfaces
2. Wipe with mineral spirits
3. Use tack cloth
4. Compressed air if available
5. Final inspection
```


2. *Final Inspection*
  Verification process:
  - Use raking light
  - Check all angles
  - Verify smoothness
  - Document surface condition

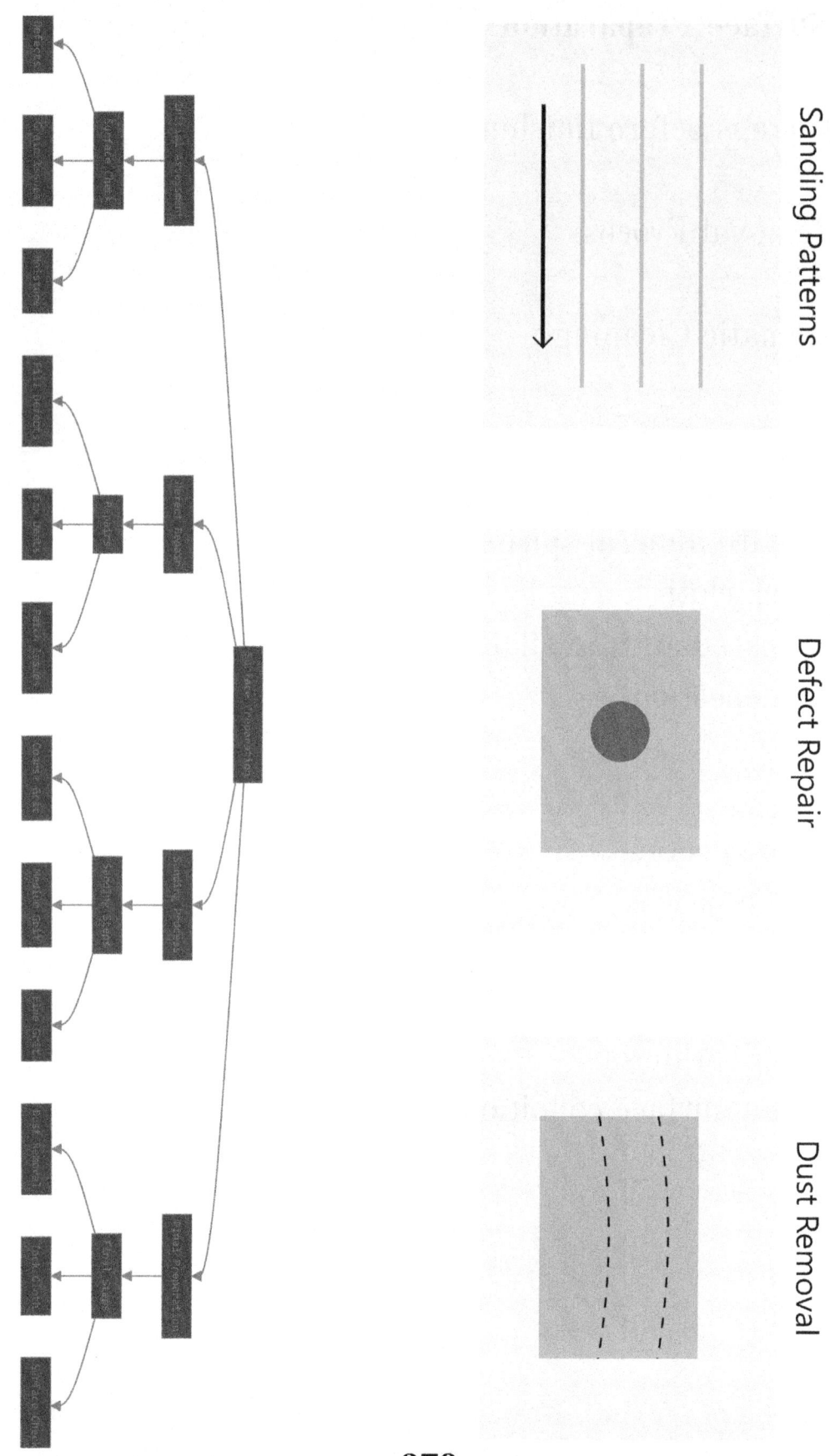

Applying Different Finishes

Let me guide you through the art and science of applying different wood finishes. Think of finish application as painting a masterpiece - each type of finish requires its own technique, and mastery comes from understanding both the materials and methods.

Environmental Preparation

Just as an artist needs the right studio conditions, proper finishing requires the right environment:

Setting Up the Finishing Area

1. *Environmental Controls*
   Optimal conditions:
   - Temperature: 65-75°F (18-24°C)
   - Humidity: 40-60%
   - Ventilation: Adequate air flow
   - Dust-free environment

   Implementation process:
   ```

   1. Clean workspace thoroughly
   2. Set up air filtration
   3. Monitor temperature/humidity
   4. Control air flow

271
   ```

5. Allow space to settle
```

## Application Techniques by Finish Type

Different finishes require specific application methods:

Oil-Based Finishes

1. *Penetrating Oils*
Application steps:
```

1. Flood surface with oil
2. Allow 15-20 minutes penetration
3. Wipe completely dry
4. Wait 24 hours between coats
5. Build up 3-4 coats minimum
```


Key technique points:
- Use lint-free cloth
- Maintain wet edge
- Watch for dry spots
- Remove all surface oil
```

2. *Oil-Based Polyurethane*
Brush application process:
``` 

1. Use high-quality brush
2. Load brush properly
3. Apply with grain
4. Maintain wet edge
5. Work in good lighting
```

Water-Based Finishes

Think of these as requiring a different rhythm than oil-based:

1. *Application Method*
Technique details:
```

1. Start with seal coat (thinned 10%)
2. Light sand between coats
3. Apply thin, even coats
4. Work quickly
5. Avoid overworking
```


2. *Layer Building*
Process steps:
- Apply seal coat

- Sand lightly (320 grit)
- Build coats (2-3)
- Final coat
- Allow full cure

Special Techniques

Advanced methods for specific situations:

French Polishing

A traditional technique for highest gloss:

1. *Building Process*
Detailed steps:
```

1. Apply shellac sealer
2. Build with pad (fad)
3. Work in circular motion
4. Gradually reduce oil
5. Final spiriting off

```

Spray Application

Modern approach for even coating:

1. *Setup Requirements*
Equipment needs:
- Proper spray equipment
- Adequate ventilation
- Correct pressure settings
- Proper material prep

2. *Technique Development*
Practice elements:
```

1. Consistent distance
2. Steady movement
3. Proper overlap
4. Even application
5. Regular pattern
```

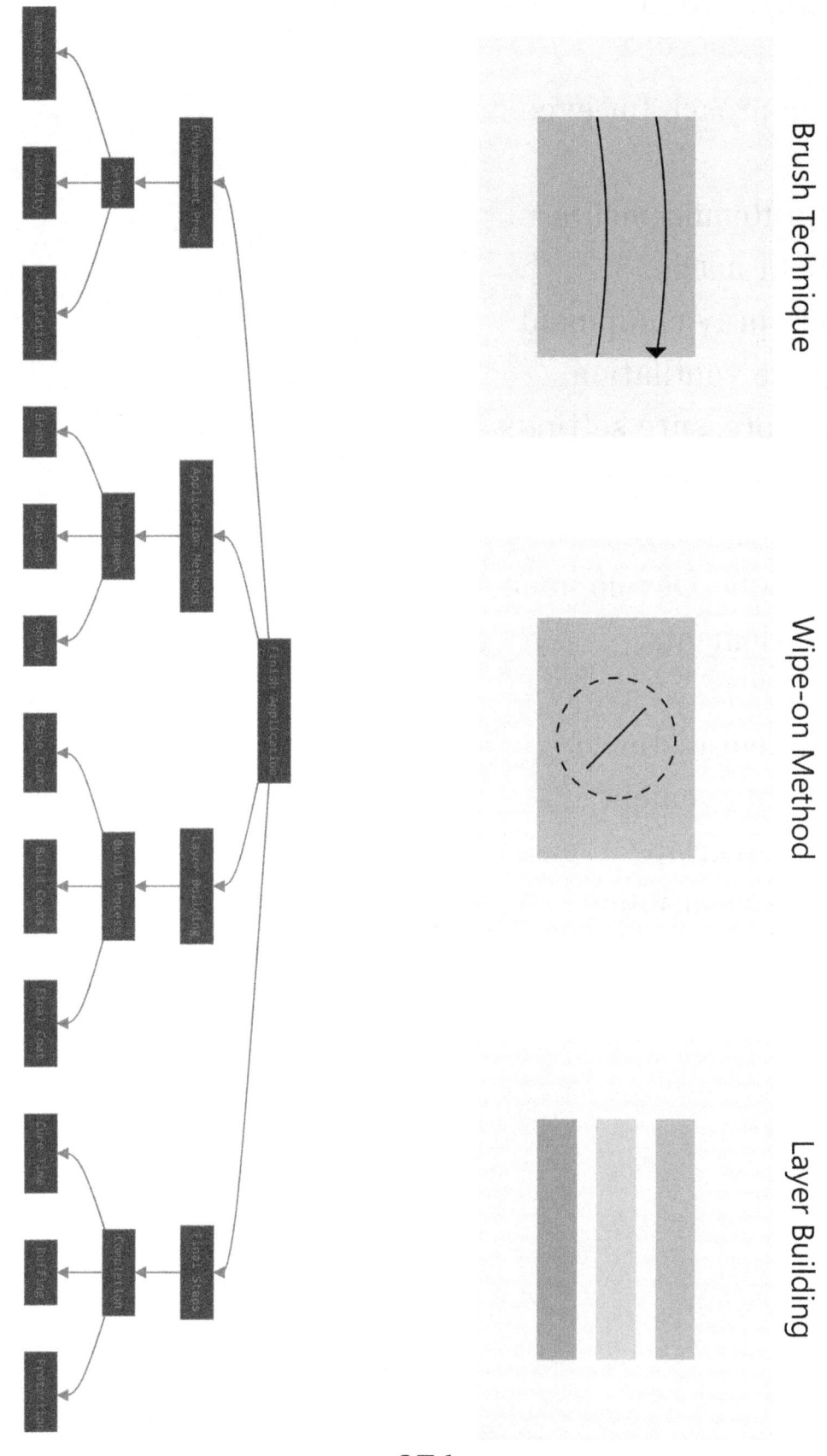

Brush Technique

Wipe-on Method

Layer Building

Protecting Your Work

Think of protecting your woodworking projects as preserving a valuable investment. Just as we take measures to protect our homes and vehicles, wooden pieces require thoughtful care to maintain their beauty and functionality over time. Let me guide you through a comprehensive approach to protecting your work.

Environmental Protection Strategies

The environment surrounding your wooden pieces plays a crucial role in their longevity:

Climate Control Fundamentals

1. *Temperature Management*
   Optimal conditions and implementation:
   ```

   Temperature Range: 65-75°F (18-24°C)
   Implementation Steps:
   1. Monitor room temperature
   2. Install thermometer
   3. Use climate control
   4. Avoid extreme fluctuations
   5. Document conditions
   ```

2. *Humidity Control*
Maintaining proper moisture levels:
``` 

Ideal Range: 40-60% relative humidity
Control Methods:
- Use hygrometer for monitoring
- Install humidifier/dehumidifier
- Maintain consistent levels
- Check seasonal changes
```


Physical Protection Methods

Direct physical protection is your first line of defense:

Surface Protection

1. *Protective Measures*
Implementation process:
```

Daily Protection:
1. Use coasters under drinks
2. Place felt pads under items
3. Apply table pads for dining
4. Use tablecloths when needed
5. Install glass tops for heavy use
```

2. *Movement Protection*
Prevent damage during use:
```

Installation Steps:
1. Add felt pads to furniture feet
2. Install bumper guards
3. Use corner protectors
4. Apply non-slip pads
5. Secure loose components
```


Maintenance Schedule Development

Regular maintenance prevents long-term issues:

Routine Care Plan

1. *Daily Care*
Basic maintenance steps:
```

Daily Tasks:
- Dust with soft cloth
- Remove spills immediately
- Check for new damage
- Adjust protective items
- Monitor environment
```

2. *Weekly Maintenance*
Deeper care routine:
``` `

Weekly Schedule:
1. Thorough cleaning
2. Inspect all surfaces
3. Check joints and hardware
4. Adjust protection as needed
5. Document any changes
``` `

Long-term Protection Strategies

Think of long-term protection as an ongoing commitment:

Annual Maintenance

1. *Yearly Assessment*
Comprehensive review:
``` `

Annual Checklist:
☐ Deep cleaning
☐ Finish inspection
☐ Hardware tightening
☐ Protection update
☐ Documentation review
``` `

2. *Refinishing Schedule*
Planning for renewal:
``` 

Evaluation Points:
1. Check finish integrity
2. Assess wear patterns
3. Document problem areas
4. Plan refinishing schedule
5. Update protection methods
```

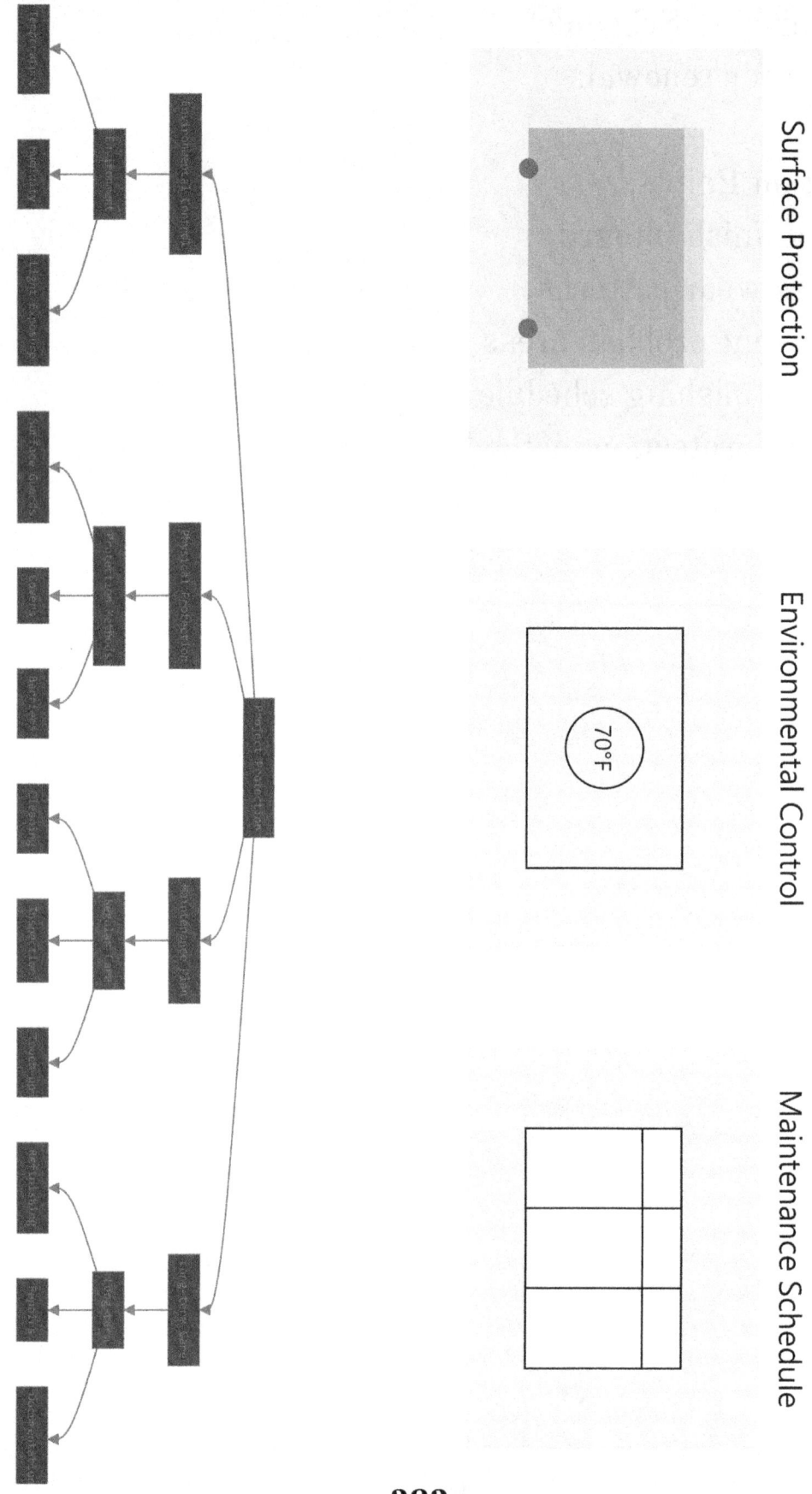

Surface Protection

Environmental Control

70°F

Maintenance Schedule

Common Finishing Problems and Solutions

Let me guide you through understanding and solving common finishing problems. Think of this as being a detective and doctor combined - first diagnosing the issue, then prescribing the right treatment. Understanding these problems and their solutions will help you achieve better finishing results and know how to fix issues when they arise.

Surface Problems and Solutions

Let's start with common surface issues that can appear during or after finishing:

Bubbles in the Finish

Think of bubbles as tiny air pockets trapped in your finish. Here's how to address them:

1. *Prevention Steps*
   Process for bubble-free application:
   ```

   Pre-Application:
   1. Allow finish to reach room temperature
   2. Stir gently, never shake
   3. Use proper brush technique
   ```

4. Work in correct temperature range

5. Apply appropriate thickness

```

2. *Correction Method*
If bubbles occur:
```

Repair Process:

1. Sand affected area with 320-grit

2. Clean thoroughly

3. Apply new coat thinly

4. Use proper technique

5. Monitor drying conditions

```

Fish Eye Problems

Fish eyes occur when surface contamination repels the finish:

1. *Identification and Prevention*
Look for:
- Small circular depressions
- Finish pulling away from spots
- Consistent pattern of defects
```

Prevention steps:
```

1. Clean surface thoroughly with solvent
2. Use fish eye eliminator additive
3. Test on scrap piece first
4. Apply seal coat if needed
```

Application Issues

Problems that occur during the application process:

Runs and Sags

Think of these as the finish losing its battle with gravity:

1. *Prevention Techniques*
Application method:
```

Proper Technique:
1. Apply thinner coats
2. Maintain consistent thickness
3. Watch for heavy edges
4. Check work angle
5. Monitor environment
```

2. *Repair Process*
When runs occur:
```

Fix Steps:
1. Allow to dry completely
2. Sand level with 320-grit
3. Clean surface thoroughly
4. Reapply finish properly
5. Monitor for recurrence
```

Environmental Problems

The environment can significantly impact your finish:

Temperature-Related Issues

1. *Cold Temperature Problems*
Issues and solutions:
```

Problems:
- Slow drying
- Poor flow
- Thick application

Solutions:
1. Warm finish to room temperature
2. Ensure proper workspace heating
```

3. Allow longer dry times
4. Consider different finish type
``` `

2. *High Temperature Issues*
Managing heat effects:
``` `

Prevention:
1. Work in cooler periods
2. Thin finish appropriately
3. Work quickly
4. Use appropriate finish type
``` `

Long-Term Problems
Issues that develop over time:

Finish Deterioration

1. *Prevention Strategies*
Long-term care:
``` `

Maintenance Plan:
1. Regular cleaning
2. Avoid harsh chemicals
3. Protect from UV exposure
4. Maintain stable environment
5. Address damage promptly

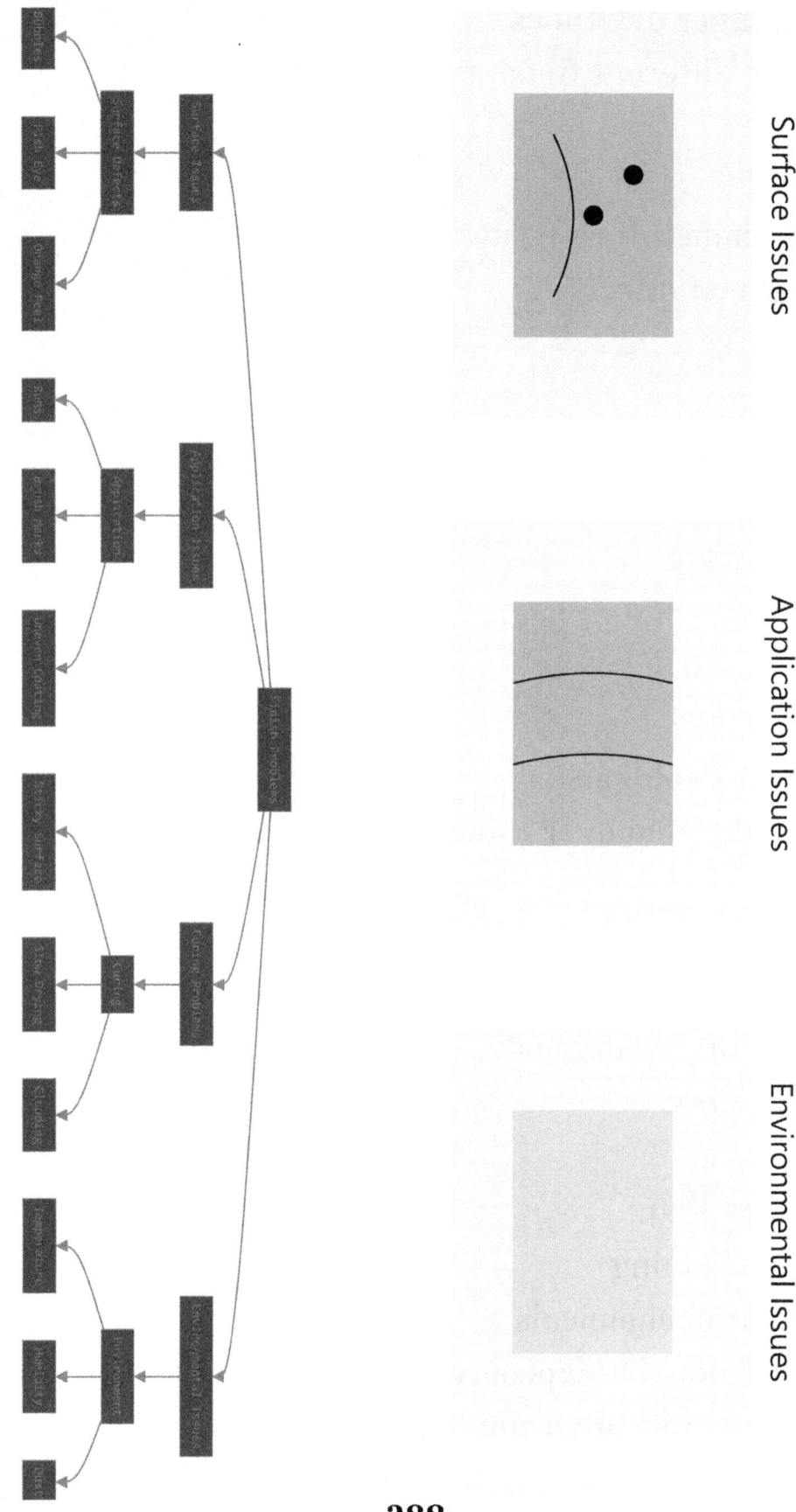

Surface Issues

Application Issues

Environmental Issues

288

Maintaining Finished Projects

Think of maintaining finished woodworking projects as caring for a valuable antique - regular attention and proper care will ensure your pieces remain beautiful and functional for generations. Let me guide you through the comprehensive process of maintaining your finished woodworking projects.

Daily Care and Maintenance

Just as we have daily routines for our personal care, finished wood pieces need regular attention to maintain their beauty and integrity.

Regular Cleaning Protocol

The foundation of good maintenance starts with proper cleaning:

1. *Daily Dusting Process*
   Implement this careful routine:
   ```

   Daily Steps:
   1. Use clean, soft microfiber cloth
   2. Wipe in direction of grain
   3. Check for new marks or damage
   4. Remove any surface debris
   ```

5. Document any concerns

Technique Details:
- Light pressure only
- No circular motions
- Replace cloth when dirty
- Avoid chemical cleaners
``` `

2. *Weekly Deep Cleaning*
More thorough maintenance approach:
``` `

Weekly Process:
1. Inspect entire piece
2. Clean with appropriate wood cleaner
3. Address any problem areas
4. Check all joints and hardware
5. Update maintenance log
``` `

Preventive Care Measures

Think of preventive care as creating a shield around your finished pieces:

Environmental Protection
```

1. *Climate Control Implementation*
Maintain optimal conditions:
``` 

Environment Checklist:
☐ Temperature: 65-75°F (18-24°C)
☐ Humidity: 40-60%
☐ Air Flow: Gentle circulation
☐ Light: Minimal direct sunlight
☐ Dust: Regular air filtering
```


2. *Physical Protection*
Implement protective measures:
```

Protection Steps:
1. Use coasters and pads
2. Install felt protectors
3. Employ table covers when needed
4. Position away from heat/AC vents
5. Regular protection assessment
```


Repair and Touch-up Procedures

Even with the best care, occasional repairs may be necessary:

Minor Repair Protocol

1. *Surface Scratches*
Address small issues promptly:
```

Repair Process:
1. Clean affected area
2. Assess damage depth
3. Choose appropriate method:
- Burnishing for light scratches
- Fill stick for deeper marks
- Touch-up marker for color
4. Blend repair area
5. Document repair
```


2. *Finish Touch-ups*
Maintain finish integrity:
```

Touch-up Steps:
1. Clean thoroughly
2. Sand lightly if needed
3. Match finish type
4. Apply thin coat
5. Allow proper drying
```

Long-term Maintenance Planning

Think of this as creating a roadmap for your piece's future:

Maintenance Schedule Development

1. *Regular Assessment Plan*
Create a systematic approach:
```

Schedule Components:
1. Daily cleaning log
2. Weekly inspection notes
3. Monthly detailed check
4. Quarterly maintenance tasks
5. Annual deep assessment
```

2. *Documentation System*
Maintain detailed records:
```

Record Keeping:
1. Maintenance activities
2. Repair history
3. Environmental conditions
4. Product usage notes
5. Future maintenance plans
```

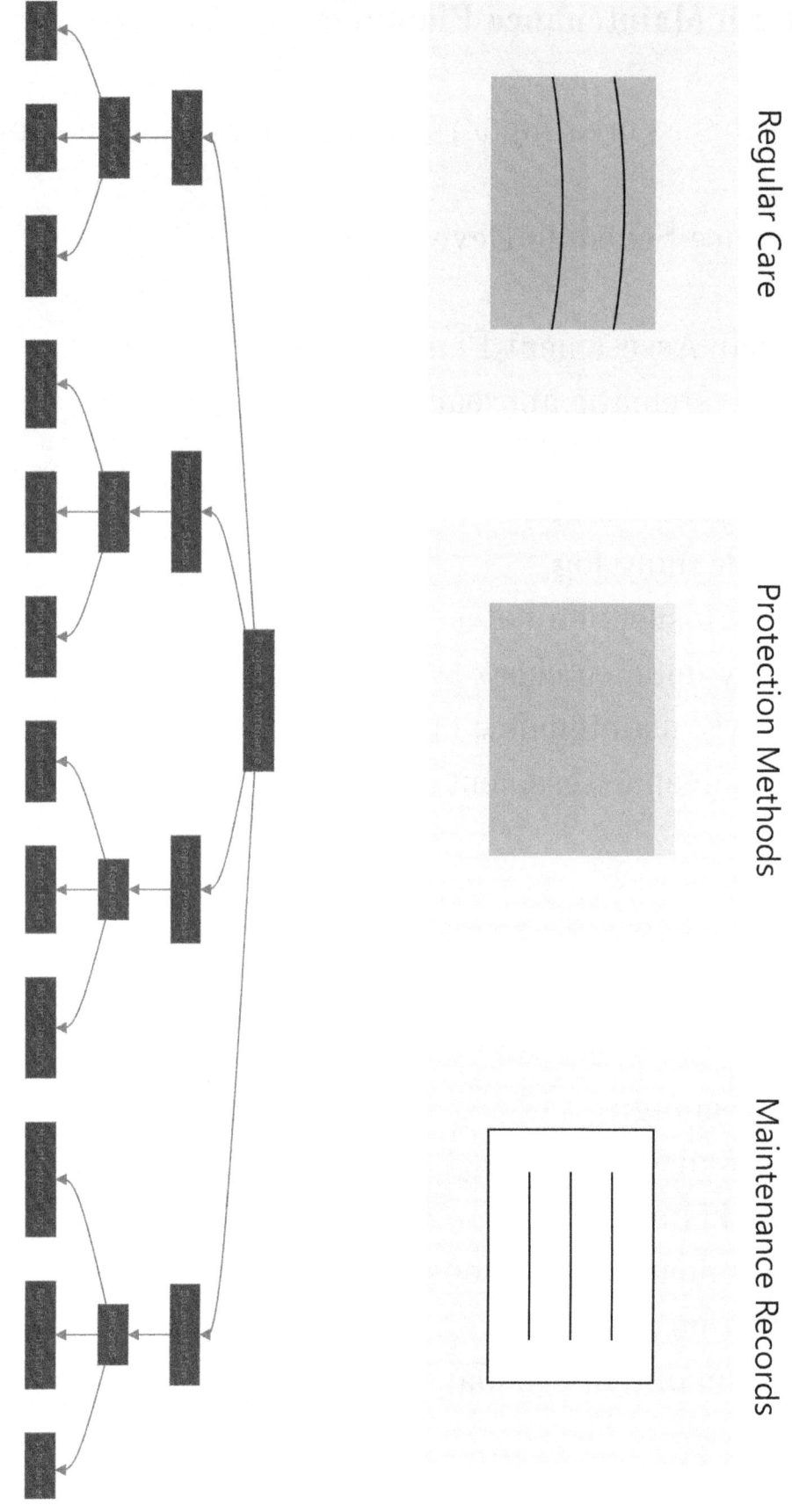

Regular Care

Protection Methods

Maintenance Records

Chapter 8
Beginner Projects

Simple Projects to Build Skills

Let me guide you through a progression of simple projects designed to build your woodworking skills systematically. Think of these projects as a ladder, where each step helps you develop specific skills while creating something useful and satisfying.

Project 1: Basic Storage Box

Our first project teaches fundamental skills while creating a practical item:

Skills Development Focus
This project introduces:
- Accurate measuring
- Straight cutting
- Basic joinery
- Assembly alignment
- Simple finishing

The process breaks down into manageable steps:

1. *Material Preparation*
``` 

Materials Needed:
- 1/2" thick wood for sides and bottom
- Wood glue
- Small nails or screws
- Sandpaper (80, 120, 220 grit)
- Finish of choice

Cut List:
2 pieces @ 8" x 4" (sides)
2 pieces @ 12" x 4" (front/back)
1 piece @ 12" x 8" (bottom)
```

2. *Assembly Process*
Step-by-step construction:
```

1. Sand all pieces to 220 grit
2. Apply glue to joints
3. Assemble sides to front/back
4. Check for square
5. Attach bottom
6. Clean glue squeeze-out
7. Final sanding
8. Apply finish
```

Project 2: Wall-Mounted Shelf

Building on basic skills, this project introduces:
- Level mounting
- Weight considerations
- Hidden fasteners
- Finish matching

Project Execution

1. *Design Considerations*
```

Planning Elements:
- Wall stud location
- Weight capacity needed
- Shelf depth and length
- Edge treatment style
- Mounting method
```

2. *Construction Steps*
Detailed process:
```

1. Cut shelf board to size
2. Shape front edge if desired
3. Sand progressively
4. Prepare mounting cleats
5. Locate and mark studs
```

6. Install mounting hardware
7. Apply finish
8. Final installation
```

**Project 3: Side Table**

This project combines previous skills and adds:
- Leg joinery
- Top flattening
- Level adjustment
- Structural integrity

Building Process

1. *Component Preparation*
```

Materials List:
- Table top: 18" x 18" x 3/4"
- Legs: 4 pieces @ 2" x 2" x 24"
- Aprons: 4 pieces @ 3" x 15"

Skills Practice:
- Square stock preparation
- Mortise and tenon joints
- Top attachment methods
- Leveling techniques
```
```

2. *Assembly Sequence*
```

Step-by-Step:
1. Prepare leg blanks
2. Cut mortises in legs
3. Create tenons on aprons
4. Test fit leg assemblies
5. Glue up base assembly
6. Attach top
7. Level and check stability
8. Final finish application
```

Skill Progression Plan

Think of these projects as building blocks:

Skill Development Track

1. *Basic Skills (Box Project)*
```

Focus Areas:
- Measuring accuracy
- Cutting straight lines
- Basic assembly
- Simple finishing
```

2. *Intermediate Skills (Shelf)*

```

```

New Techniques:
- Edge treatments
- Hardware installation
- Wall mounting
- Finish matching

```

```

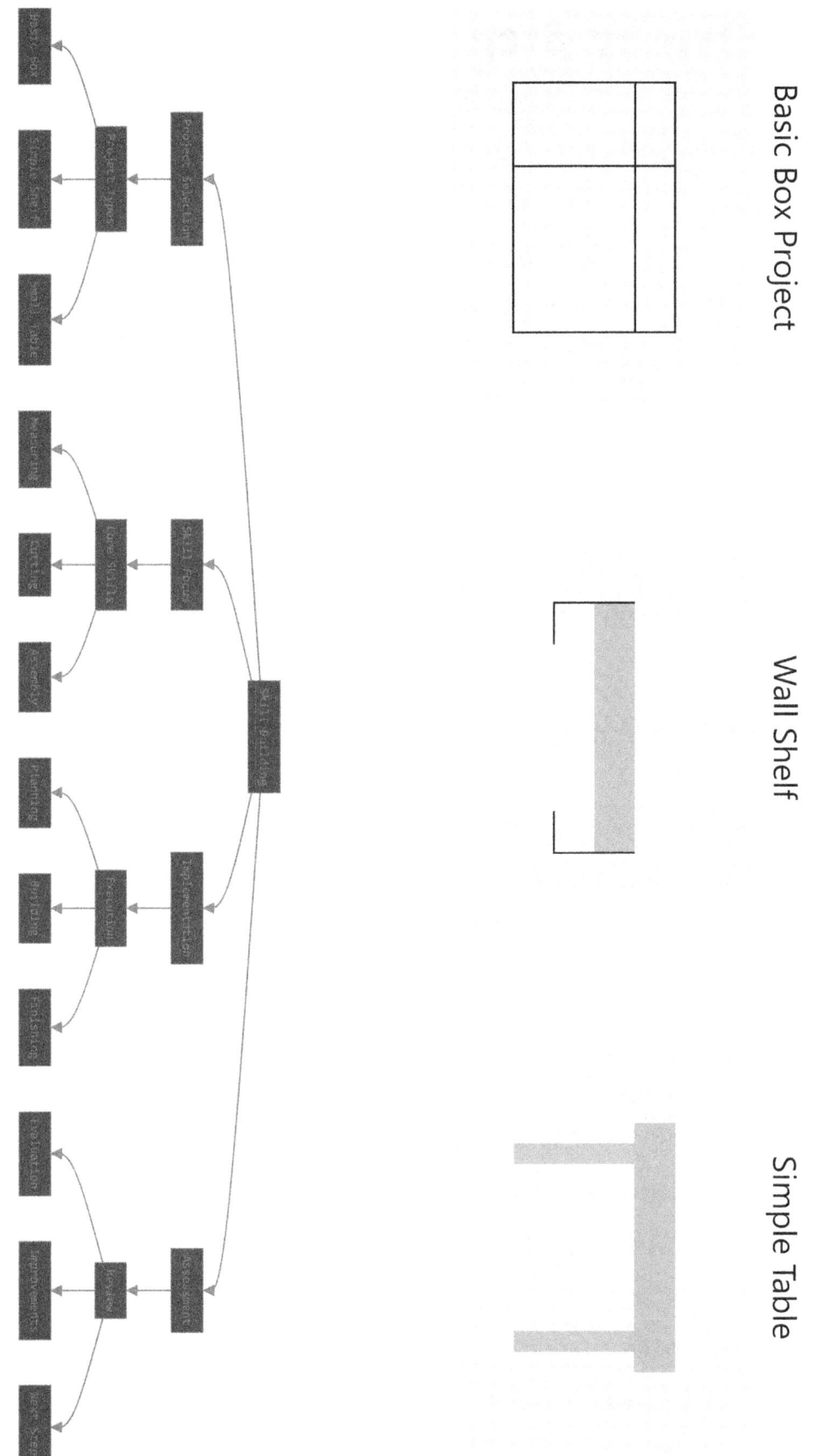

Basic Box Project

Wall Shelf

Simple Table

301

Step-by-Step Project Guides

Let me guide you through creating comprehensive project guides that will ensure success in your woodworking endeavors. Think of a project guide as a detailed roadmap that not only shows you where you're going but explains every turn along the way.

Phase 1: Project Planning

The foundation of any successful project lies in thorough planning. Let's break this down into manageable steps:

Initial Project Documentation

1. *Project Overview Development*
   Create a detailed project brief:
   ```

   Project Documentation:
   1. Project name and description
   2. Final dimensions
   3. Intended use/location
   4. Special requirements
   5. Timeline expectations

   Key Considerations:
   - Skill level requirements
   - Tool availability
   ```

- Space constraints
- Budget limitations
``` ` ` ` ```

2. *Materials and Tools List*
Comprehensive inventory preparation:
``` ` ` ` ```

Materials Documentation:
☐ Primary wood species and quantities
☐ Secondary materials
☐ Hardware requirements
☐ Finishing supplies
☐ Safety equipment

Tools Checklist:
☐ Hand tools needed
☐ Power tools required
☐ Measuring/marking tools
☐ Specialty tools
☐ Safety equipment
``` ` ` ` ```

Phase 2: Step-by-Step Process Development

Break down the project into clear, manageable steps:

Component Creation Sequence
```

1. *Stock Preparation Steps*
Detailed process guide:
```

Step 1: Rough Cutting
- Cut stock slightly oversized
- Allow for cleanup
- Mark reference faces
- Document dimensions

Step 2: Milling Process
- Face jointing
- Edge jointing
- Thickness planing
- Final dimensioning
```


2. *Assembly Sequence*
Clear order of operations:
```

Assembly Steps:
1. Dry fit all components
2. Mark joint locations
3. Prepare joinery
4. Test fit assemblies
5. Final glue-up sequence
```

Phase 3: Quality Control Integration

Build quality checks into each step:

Quality Checkpoints

1. *Measurement Verification*
Regular checking process:
```

Verification Steps:
☐ Compare to plans
☐ Check square/parallel
☐ Verify dimensions
☐ Test fit components
☐ Document variances
```


2. *Progress Documentation*
Keep detailed records:
```

Documentation Points:
1. Photos of key steps
2. Measurement notes
3. Process modifications
4. Problem solutions
5. Time tracking
```

Phase 4: Troubleshooting Integration

Prepare for potential issues:

Problem-Solving Framework

1. *Common Issues Section*
Address potential problems:
```

Problem Categories:
- Material issues
- Tool problems
- Assembly challenges
- Finishing concerns

Each Entry Includes:
- Problem description
- Potential causes
- Solution options
- Prevention methods
```

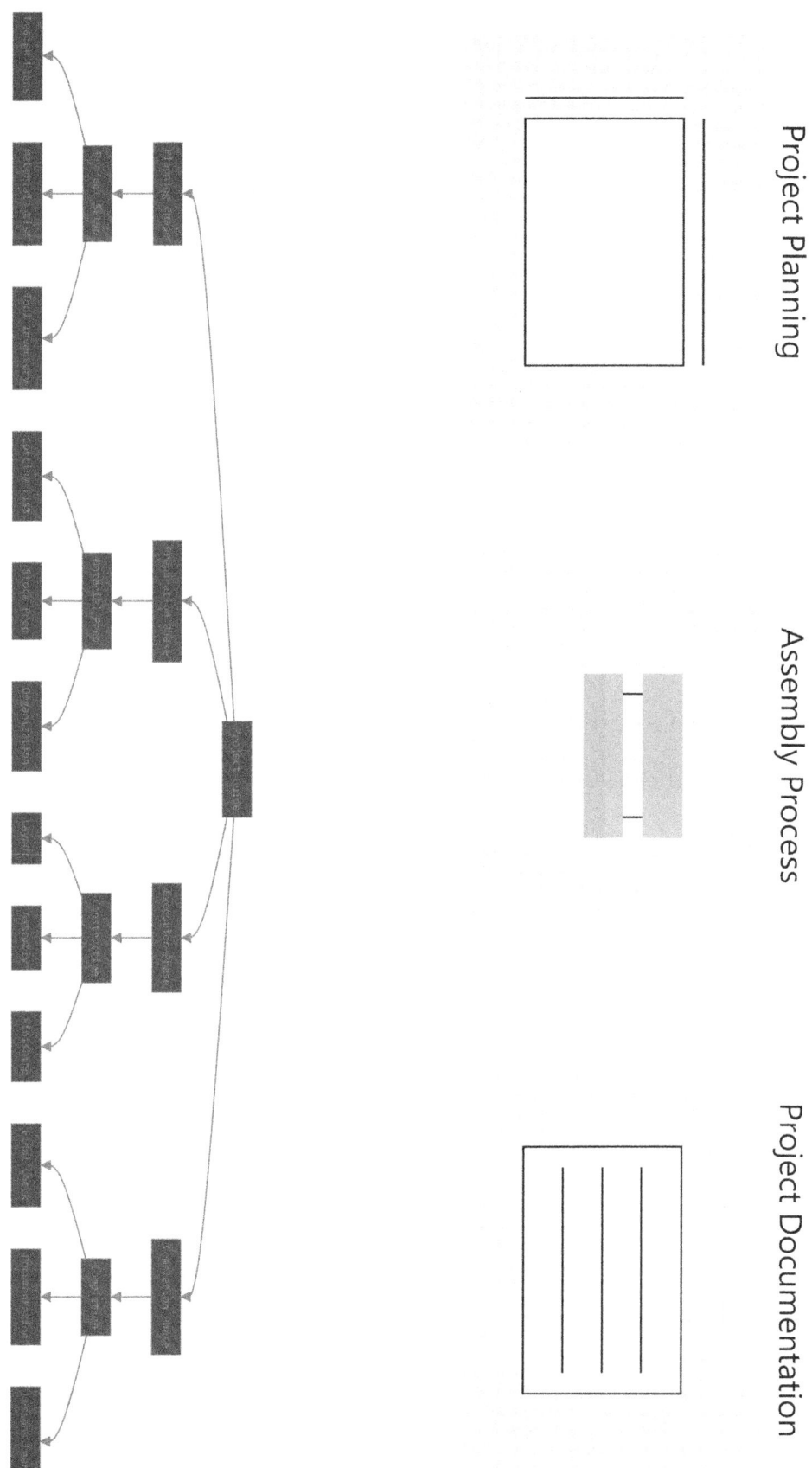

Project Planning

Assembly Process

Project Documentation

Problem-Solving Through Practice

Let me guide you through developing effective problem-solving skills through deliberate practice in woodworking. Think of this process as building a toolkit of solutions that grows with each challenge you encounter and overcome.

Building a Strong Foundation

Begin by establishing core problem-solving capabilities:

Basic Skill Development

1. *Fundamental Skills Practice*
   Create a structured practice routine:
   ```

   Daily Practice Schedule:
   Morning Session (1 hour):
   - Measuring exercises (15 min)
   - Cutting practice (20 min)
   - Joint creation (25 min)

   Focus Areas:
   ☐ Accuracy in measurement
   ☐ Consistency in cutting
   ☐ Clean joint creation
   ☐ Tool control mastery
   ```

2. *Progressive Challenge System*
Develop skills systematically:
``` 

Skill Progression:
Level 1: Basic cuts and joints
- Straight cuts
- Simple joints
- Basic measurements

Level 2: Complex operations
- Compound angles
- Complex joinery
- Precise fitting
```

Structured Practice Methods

Implement specific practice techniques:

Deliberate Practice Approach

1. *Focused Practice Sessions*
Design targeted exercises:
```

Practice Project Structure:
1. Select specific skill focus
2. Create practice pieces
3. Evaluate results
```

4. Document learning
5. Adjust technique

Time Management:
- 25-minute focused sessions
- 5-minute evaluation periods
- Progressive difficulty
``` 


2. *Error Analysis and Correction*
Learn from mistakes systematically:
``` 

Error Assessment Process:
1. Identify error type
2. Analyze cause
3. Test solutions
4. Document findings
5. Create prevention strategy
``` 


**Problem-Solving Methodology**

Develop a systematic approach to challenges:

Analysis Framework

1. *Problem Identification*
Create detailed analysis:
```

Assessment Questions:
- What is the exact issue?
- When did it first appear?
- What preceded the problem?
- What are the symptoms?
- What has changed?
```


2. *Solution Development*
Build solution strategies:
```

Solution Process:
1. List possible approaches
2. Evaluate each option
3. Test selected method
4. Document results
5. Refine approach
```


## Progress Tracking and Evaluation

Monitor and document your growth:

Documentation System

1. *Progress Journal*
Keep detailed records:
```

Journal Entries Include:
- Date and time
- Skills practiced
- Challenges faced
- Solutions found
- Lessons learned

Review Schedule:
- Daily entries
- Weekly review
- Monthly assessment
- Quarterly planning
```


2. *Skill Assessment*
Regular evaluation process:
```

Assessment Areas:
☐ Technical accuracy
☐ Time efficiency
☐ Problem-solving speed
☐ Solution quality
☐ Tool proficiency
```
```

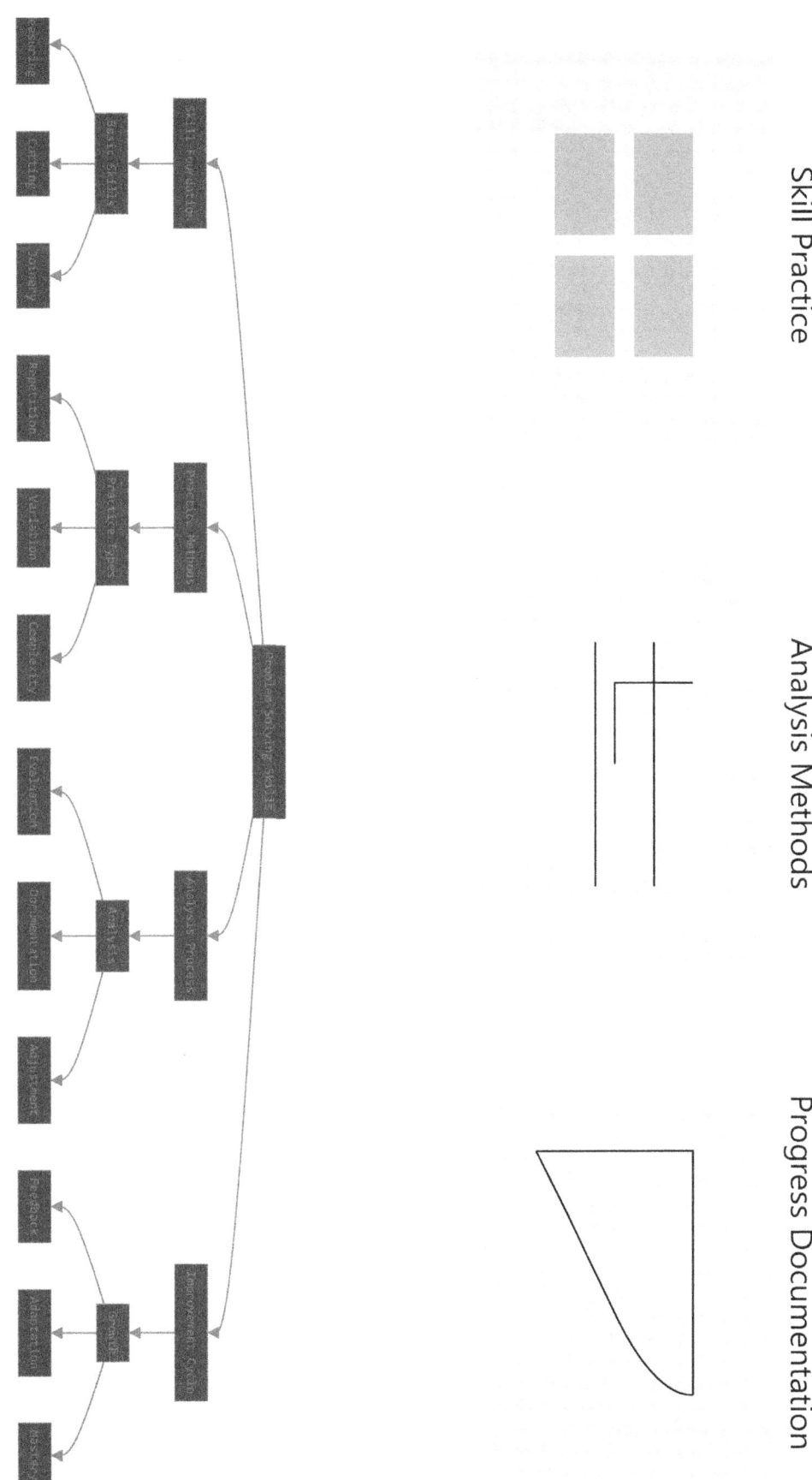

Skill Practice

Analysis Methods

Progress Documentation

Building Confidence Through Success

Let me guide you through the process of building confidence in your woodworking journey through systematic success-building strategies. Think of confidence building as constructing a sturdy house - it requires a solid foundation, careful planning, and gradual progress through achievable steps.

Foundation Building Phase

Start by establishing a strong base of basic skills and small victories:

Creating Early Successes

1. *Simple Project Selection*
   Choose projects that guarantee early wins:
   ```

   Project Progression:
   Week 1-2: Basic cutting board
   - Simple straight cuts
   - Basic glue-up
   - Surface finishing

   Week 3-4: Small box
   - Square corners
   ```

- Simple joinery
- Hardware installation

Documentation:
☐ Photos of completed projects
☐ Notes on lessons learned
☐ Skills mastered
☐ Challenges overcome
```


2. *Skill Building Sequence*
Develop abilities systematically:
```

Basic Skills Checklist:
1. Measuring accuracy ($\pm 1/32$")
2. Straight cutting (within pencil line)
3. Square assembly (check diagonals)
4. Clean glue-ups (minimal squeeze-out)
5. Smooth finishing (no runs)
```


## Progress Tracking and Celebration

Document and celebrate achievements:

Achievement Recognition System
```

1. *Progress Documentation*
Create a detailed record:
` ` `

Project Journal Format:
Entry Components:
- Project name and date
- Skills employed
- Challenges faced
- Solutions found
- Photos of process
- Final outcome

Review Schedule:
- Daily progress notes
- Weekly achievement review
- Monthly skill assessment
- Quarterly goal setting
` ` `

2. *Success Celebration*
Acknowledge achievements:
` ` `

Recognition Methods:
☐ Photo gallery of projects
☐ Skills mastery chart
☐ Project complexity progression
☐ Technique improvement tracking
` ` `

Confidence Building Techniques

Develop mental strength alongside physical skills:

Positive Reinforcement Methods

1. *Self-Assessment Tools*
Regular evaluation process:
```

Weekly Review Questions:
1. What went well this week?
2. Which skills improved?
3. What challenges were overcome?
4. What new techniques were learned?
5. What's the next achievement goal?
```


2. *Growth Mindset Development*
Cultivate positive thinking:
```

Daily Practice:
- Acknowledge small improvements
- Learn from mistakes
- Focus on progress
- Set achievable goals
- Celebrate effort
```

Structured Growth Path

Create a clear progression plan:

Skill Development Timeline

1. *Monthly Goals*
Set achievable targets:
```

Month 1: Fundamental Skills
- Accurate measuring
- Clean cutting
- Basic joinery

Month 2: Project Completion
- Simple box construction
- Basic finishing
- Hardware installation

Month 3: Advanced Techniques
- Complex joinery
- Detail work
- Project design
```

2. *Challenge Integration*
Gradually increase difficulty:
``` 

Challenge Progression:
Level 1: Basic Skills
- Straight cuts
- Simple joints
- Basic assembly

Level 2: Intermediate
- Compound angles
- Complex joinery
- Project design

Level 3: Advanced
- Original designs
- Specialty techniques
- Teaching others
```

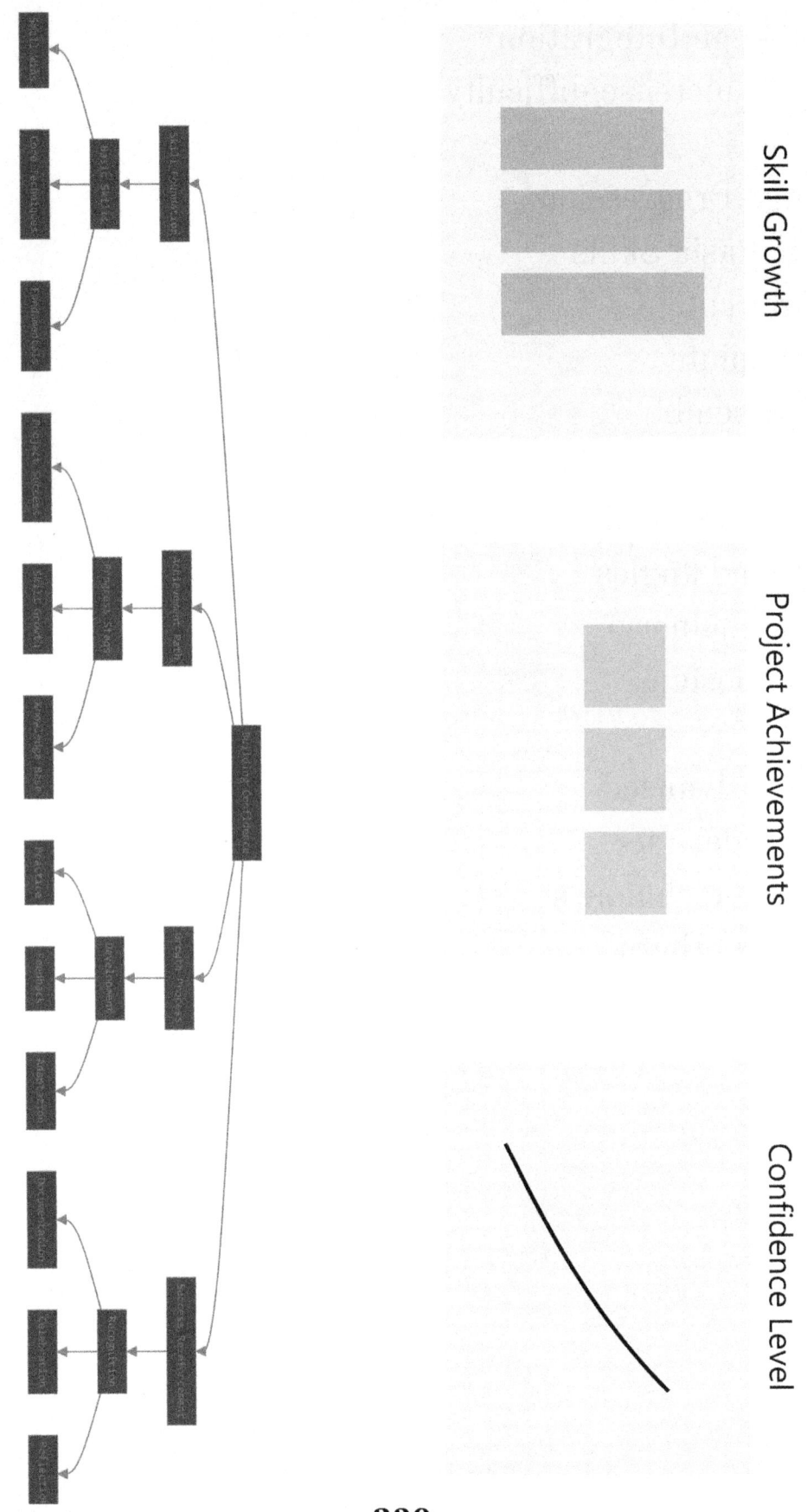

Skill Growth

Project Achievements

Confidence Level

Project Modifications and Adaptations

Let me guide you through the process of effectively modifying and adapting woodworking projects. Think of project modifications as being like tailoring a suit - you start with a basic pattern but adjust it to fit specific needs and preferences while maintaining structural integrity and functionality.

Initial Assessment Phase

Before making any modifications, we need to thoroughly understand both the original design and desired changes:

Design Analysis

1. *Original Project Evaluation*
   Create a detailed assessment:
   ```

   Analysis Components:
   1. Critical Dimensions
   - Load-bearing elements
   - Joint locations
   - Material thicknesses

   2. Structural Elements
   - Support mechanisms
   ```

- Weight distribution
- Stress points

3. Material Properties
- Wood species characteristics
- Grain orientation
- Moisture considerations
``` `

2. *Modification Requirements*
Document needed changes:
``` `

Change Documentation:
☐ Size adjustments needed
☐ Functional modifications
☐ Aesthetic alterations
☐ Material substitutions
☐ Construction method changes
``` `

Planning Modifications

Develop a systematic approach to implementing changes:

Modification Strategy

1. *Design Changes*
Structure your modifications:
``` ` **322**

Design Process:
1. Create scaled drawings
2. Identify affected components
3. Evaluate structural impact
4. Develop new joint details
5. Update cut lists

Documentation:
- Original dimensions
- Modified dimensions
- Changed angles
- New joinery details
```


2. *Material Adaptations*
Plan material changes:
```

Material Considerations:
1. Strength requirements
- Original specifications
- New requirements
- Safety factors

2. Aesthetic impact
- Color matching
- Grain patterns
- Finish compatibility
```
```

Implementation Process

Execute modifications systematically:

Modification Execution

1. *Step-by-Step Implementation*
Follow organized process:
```

Implementation Sequence:
1. Prepare workspace
- Layout modified plans
- Gather new materials
- Set up tools

2. Execute changes
- Follow modification sequence
- Check measurements frequently
- Document alterations
- Test fit components
```

2. *Quality Control*
Maintain standards:
```

Quality Checkpoints:
☐ Measure twice, cut once
☐ Test joints before assembly
```

☐ Check square and level
☐ Verify specifications
☐ Document variations
``` 


## Testing and Verification

Ensure modifications meet requirements:

Testing Process

1. *Functional Testing*
Verify modifications:
``` 

Test Categories:
1. Structural integrity
- Load testing
- Joint stability
- Balance check

2. Functionality
- Movement check
- Operation test
- Fit verification
```
```

2. *Documentation*
Record results:
```

Documentation Elements:
- Photos before/after
- Measurement records
- Change notes
- Test results
- Future recommendations
```

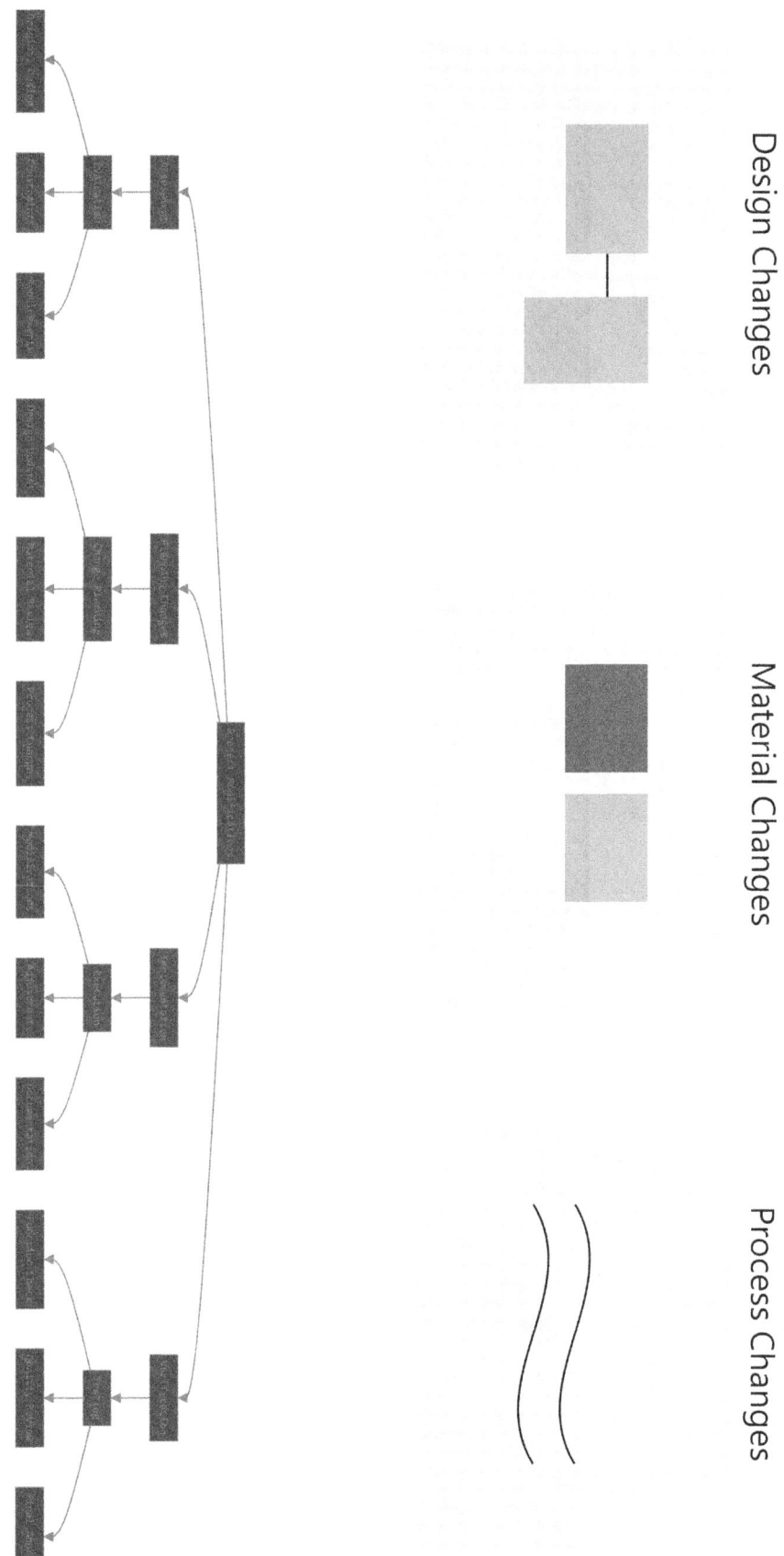

Design Changes

Material Changes

Process Changes

327

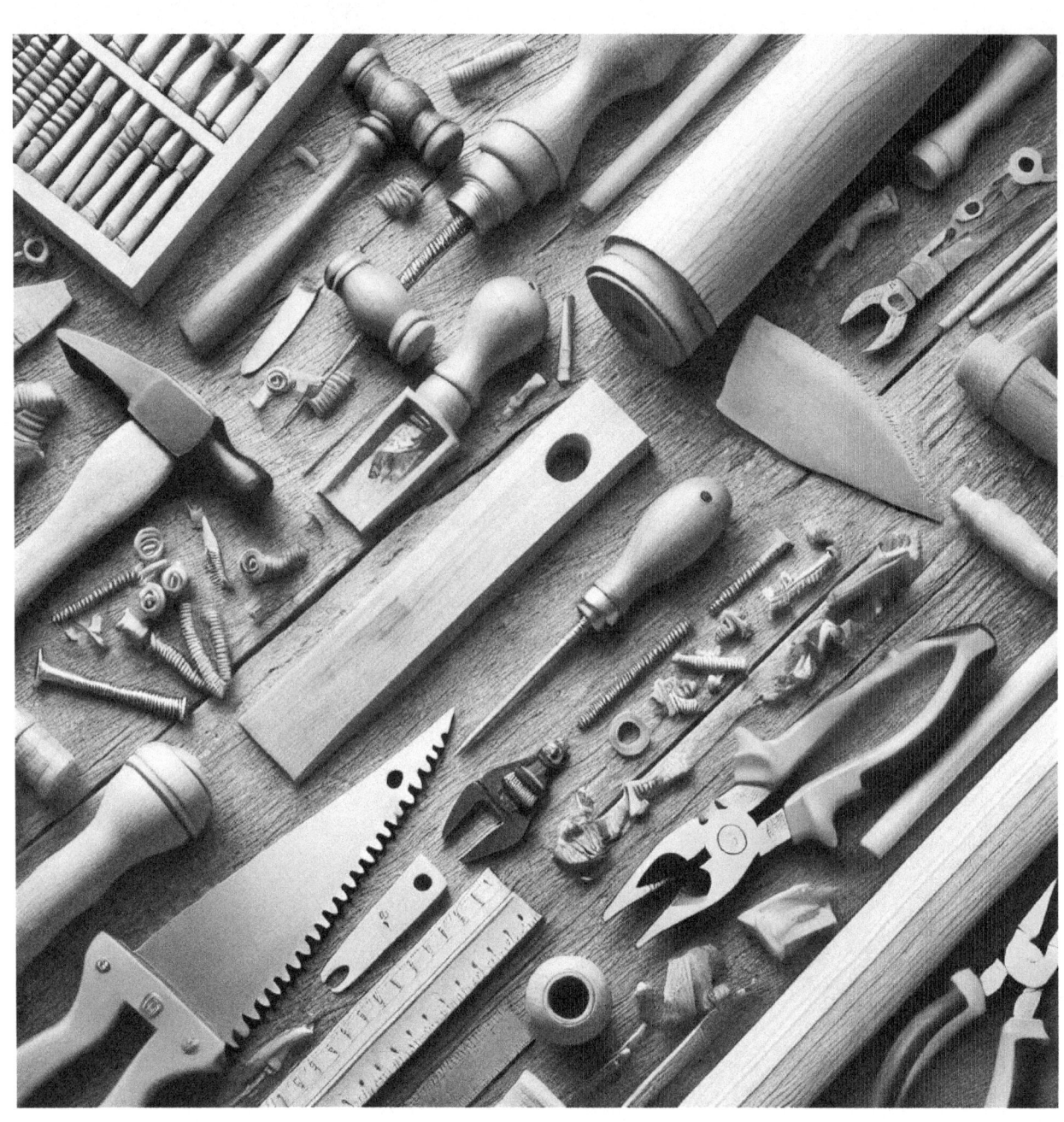

328

Appendices

Wood Species Reference Guide

Let me guide you through a comprehensive understanding of wood species commonly used in woodworking. Think of this guide as a botanical field guide specifically tailored for woodworkers, helping you understand not just what each wood looks like, but how it behaves and performs in your projects.

Hardwoods

Oak (Quercus species)
White Oak stands as one of woodworking's most versatile materials. Imagine a wood that combines the strength of steel with the warmth of nature. Its tight grain pattern creates a natural resistance to water, which explains why it has been used in shipbuilding for centuries. When working with White Oak, you'll notice its distinctive ray fleck pattern – those shimmering lines that appear when quarter sawn – creating what we call figure in the wood.

Working characteristics:
- Density: 47 lbs/cubic foot
- Janka hardness: 1,360 lbf
- Seasonal movement: Moderate

Red Oak, while similar to its white cousin, brings its own characteristics to your workshop. Its more porous nature makes it less suitable for outdoor projects, but its rich, warm color and excellent staining properties make it a favorite for interior furniture. When cutting Red Oak, you'll find it responds well to both hand and power tools, though its open grain structure requires careful attention during finishing.

Maple (Acer species)

Hard Maple, also known as Sugar Maple, presents itself as nature's answer to everyday wear and tear. Picture a wood so dense and hard that it's commonly used for bowling alley lanes. Its tight, uniform grain pattern creates a surface that resists marking and maintains its appearance even under heavy use. When working with Hard Maple, you'll need sharp tools and patience – its density can make it challenging to work with hand tools.

Consider its characteristics:
- Density: 44 lbs/cubic foot
- Janka hardness: 1,450 lbf
- Seasonal movement: High

Soft Maple, despite its name, still proves harder than many other hardwoods. Think of it as Hard Maple's more approachable sibling – easier to work with while still maintaining excellent durability.

Its lighter color and easier workability make it perfect for painted furniture and architectural millwork.

Softwoods

Pine (Pinus species)

Eastern White Pine serves as an excellent introduction to woodworking. Imagine working with a material that forgives small mistakes while teaching you the fundamentals of wood behavior. Its soft nature allows you to easily see how your tools interact with the wood grain, making it an ideal learning material. However, don't mistake its softness for weakness – properly finished and maintained, Pine furniture can last for generations.

Key properties:
- Density: 25 lbs/cubic foot
- Janka hardness: 380 lbf
- Seasonal movement: Low to moderate

Southern Yellow Pine presents a different character altogether. Despite being a softwood, it often rivals some hardwoods in density and strength. When working with Southern Yellow Pine, you'll notice its pronounced grain pattern and significant density variation between early and latewood, which can affect how it machines and finishes.

Cedar (Thuja species)

Western Red Cedar embodies nature's own preservation system. This remarkable wood contains natural compounds that resist decay and insect attack, making it ideal for outdoor projects. When working with Cedar, you'll notice its distinctive fragrance – a pleasant reminder of its natural protective properties. Its straight grain and uniform texture make it exceptionally stable and easy to work with, though its softness requires careful handling to avoid denting.

Important considerations:
- Density: 23 lbs/cubic foot
- Janka hardness: 350 lbf
- Seasonal movement: Very low

Exotic Woods

Mahogany (Swietenia macrophylla)

Genuine Mahogany represents the gold standard in furniture woods. Working with Mahogany feels like a partnership between craftsperson and material – it cuts cleanly, holds detail well, and remains stable after machining. Its reddish-brown color deepens with age, creating furniture that becomes more beautiful over time. When selecting Mahogany, you'll notice its straight grain and uniform texture, qualities that make it particularly forgiving to work with.

Properties to consider:
- Density: 35 lbs/cubic foot
- Janka hardness: 800 lbf
- Seasonal movement: Low

Teak (Tectona grandis)

Think of Teak as nature's weatherproof wood. Its high oil content and dense grain structure create a natural resistance to water, decay, and insects. Working with Teak requires respect for its silica content, which can dull tools quickly, but the results justify the extra effort. Its golden-brown color and excellent stability make it particularly valued for outdoor furniture and marine applications.

Tool Shopping Guide

Let me guide you through the process of building your woodworking tool collection thoughtfully and efficiently. Think of this guide as your personal advisor for making informed decisions about tool investments, helping you build a workshop that grows with your skills.

Understanding Tool Quality Levels

When we talk about woodworking tools, imagine them existing on a spectrum from entry-level to professional grade. Just as a chef progresses from basic kitchen knives to professional cutlery, woodworkers typically advance through different tool quality levels as their skills develop.

Entry-Level Tools

These tools serve as your introduction to woodworking, much like training wheels on a bicycle. They should be affordable yet functional enough to help you learn proper technique. Consider spending about 40-60% of professional-grade tool prices at this level.

For example, when choosing your first hand plane, look for these characteristics:
- Ductile iron construction (rather than pot metal)
- Adjustable blade mechanism
- Reasonable flatness (within 0.005" across the sole)

- Replaceable blades
- Basic adjustment features

Entry-level brands worth considering include:
- Stanley for basic hand tools
- Ryobi for power tools
- Buck Bros for chisels
- Irwin for measuring and marking tools

Mid-Range Tools

Think of these as your "growing phase" tools. They offer better performance and longevity without requiring professional-level investment. These tools typically cost 60-80% of professional-grade prices.

Key features to look for:
- Machined surfaces rather than cast
- Better materials (high-carbon steel vs basic steel)
- More precise adjustment mechanisms
- Longer warranties
- Better overall fit and finish

Recommended mid-range brands include:
- Veritas for hand planes
- DeWalt for power tools
- Narex for chisels
- Incra for precision measuring tools

Professional-Grade Tools

Consider these lifetime investments. They offer the highest precision, durability, and refined features. While expensive, they often prove cost-effective over time through superior performance and longevity.

Characteristics worth the investment:
- Premium materials throughout
- Highest precision manufacturing
- Finest adjustment capabilities
- Lifetime warranties
- Superior ergonomics

Notable professional brands include:
- Lie-Nielsen for hand planes
- Festool for power tools
- Ashley Iles for chisels
- Bridge City Tool Works for precision tools

Essential First Purchases

Let's start with the fundamental tools that form the foundation of your workshop. Think of these as your woodworking alphabet – the basic elements from which all projects begin.

Measuring and Marking
Start with:
1. Combination Square (12-inch)
- Expected investment: $30-60
- Look for machined surfaces
- Check for square accuracy
- Verify smooth slider operation

2. Marking Knife
- Expected investment: $15-30
- High-carbon steel blade
- Comfortable handle
- Good balance

Cutting Tools
Begin with:
1. Hand Saw
- Expected investment: $40-80
- Sharp teeth, minimal set
- Comfortable handle
- Good tension in blade

2. Chisels (basic set)
- Expected investment: $50-100
- High-carbon steel
- Good edge retention
- Comfortable handles

Tool Buying Strategy

Think of building your tool collection as creating a well-planned garden – start with essentials and expand thoughtfully.

Prioritization Method
Consider these factors when deciding what to buy:
1. Immediate project needs
  - What tools are absolutely necessary?
  - Can any tools serve multiple purposes?
  - Which processes can't be done without specific tools?

2. Skill development requirements
  - Which tools help build fundamental skills?
  - What tools offer room for technique improvement?
  - Which tools teach important woodworking principles?

3. Budget allocation
  - Spend more on frequently used tools
  - Invest in quality for precision tools
  - Consider long-term value over initial cost

Where to Buy
Different purchasing venues offer various advantages:

1. Local Woodworking Stores
Benefits:
- Hands-on inspection
- Expert advice
- Immediate availability
- Building relationships with experts

2. Online Retailers
Advantages:
- Wider selection
- Competitive pricing
- Detailed reviews
- Easy comparison shopping

3. Used Tools
Considerations:
- Significant cost savings
- Potential for high-quality vintage tools
- Requires knowledge to evaluate condition
- May need restoration work

Measurement Conversion Charts

Let me take you through the essential measurement conversions you'll encounter in woodworking, breaking them down into easily understandable relationships. Think of these conversions as a translation guide between different "languages" of measurement – each with its own strengths and specific uses in woodworking.

Imperial to Metric Length Conversions

Understanding the relationship between inches and millimeters forms the foundation of measurement conversion. Let's break this down into commonly used increments:

Inches to Millimeters (Basic Units):
```

1/16 inch = 1.588 mm
1/8 inch = 3.175 mm
1/4 inch = 6.35 mm
3/8 inch = 9.525 mm
1/2 inch = 12.7 mm
3/4 inch = 19.05 mm
1 inch = 25.4 mm
```

For longer measurements, consider these common woodworking dimensions:

```

2 inches = 50.8 mm
3 inches = 76.2 mm
4 inches = 101.6 mm
6 inches = 152.4 mm
12 inches (1 foot) = 304.8 mm
24 inches (2 feet) = 609.6 mm
36 inches (3 feet) = 914.4 mm
48 inches (4 feet) = 1219.2 mm
```


Common Fractions to Decimals

In woodworking, you'll often need to convert between fractional and decimal measurements, especially when using digital tools. Here's a comprehensive conversion chart:

```

1/64 = 0.015625
1/32 = 0.03125
3/64 = 0.046875
1/16 = 0.0625
5/64 = 0.078125
3/32 = 0.09375
7/64 = 0.109375
1/8 = 0.125
```

9/64 = 0.140625
5/32 = 0.15625
11/64 = 0.171875
3/16 = 0.1875
13/64 = 0.203125
7/32 = 0.21875
15/64 = 0.234375
1/4 = 0.25
` ` `

Board Foot Calculations

Understanding board feet helps in material purchasing and project planning. The basic formula is:
` ` `

Board Feet = (Thickness in inches $\times$ Width in inches $\times$ Length in feet) $\div$ 12
` ` `

Common conversions for 4/4 (1-inch thick) lumber:
` ` `

1$\times$4 $\times$ 8 feet = 2.67 board feet
1$\times$6 $\times$ 8 feet = 4 board feet
1$\times$8 $\times$ 8 feet = 5.33 board feet
1$\times$10 $\times$ 8 feet = 6.67 board feet
1$\times$12 $\times$ 8 feet = 8 board feet
` ` `

Area Conversions

When working with sheet goods or calculating surface area, these conversions prove invaluable:

Square Inches to Square Centimeters:
```

1 square inch = 6.4516 square centimeters
4 square inches = 25.8064 square centimeters
9 square inches = 58.0644 square centimeters
16 square inches = 103.2258 square centimeters
```


Common Sheet Good Sizes:
```

$2 \times 2$ feet = 0.3716 square meters
$2 \times 4$ feet = 0.7432 square meters
$4 \times 4$ feet = 1.4864 square meters
$4 \times 8$ feet = 2.9728 square meters
```


Temperature Conversions

Understanding temperature becomes crucial when working with finishes and adhesives:

```
```

Fahrenheit to Celsius Formula:
$$°C = (°F - 32) \times 5/9$$

Common Workshop Temperatures:
65°F = 18.3°C (Minimum working temperature)
70°F = 21.1°C (Ideal working temperature)
75°F = 23.9°C (Maximum recommended for most finishes)
```
```

Weight Conversions

Useful for material handling and shipping calculations:

```
```

Pounds to Kilograms:
1 pound = 0.4536 kilograms
2 pounds = 0.9072 kilograms
5 pounds = 2.2680 kilograms
10 pounds = 4.5359 kilograms
20 pounds = 9.0718 kilograms
50 pounds = 22.6796 kilograms
100 pounds = 45.3592 kilograms
```
```

Safety Checklist

Think of workshop safety as building a protective shield around yourself - each safety measure adds another layer of protection. Let me guide you through creating a comprehensive safety environment in your workshop, explaining not just what to do, but why each measure matters.

Personal Protective Equipment (PPE)

Your first line of defense begins with proper personal protection. Consider these items as your workshop armor:

Eye Protection
Before starting any woodworking activity, ensure:
- Safety glasses meet ANSI Z87.1 standards
- Glasses fit properly and comfortably
- Lenses are clean and scratch-free
- Side shields are in place
- Prescription safety glasses if needed
- Face shield available for heavy debris work

Understanding proper use is crucial: Always wear eye protection even for "quick cuts" - many accidents happen during brief tasks when we let our guard down. Keep multiple pairs accessible throughout your workshop, creating no excuse for working without protection.

Hearing Protection
Protect your hearing with these essential steps:
- Use ear protection when noise exceeds 85 decibels
- Ensure proper fit of earplugs or earmuffs
- Replace disposable protection regularly
- Clean reusable protection after use
- Consider dual protection for extremely loud operations
- Keep spare hearing protection readily available

Remember that hearing damage is cumulative and irreversible. When in doubt about noise levels, err on the side of protection.

Workshop Environment

Creating a safe working environment requires attention to several key areas:

Lighting and Visibility
Ensure proper illumination:
- All work areas well-lit without shadows
- Task lighting available for detail work
- No flickering lights that could cause strobe effect
- Emergency lighting operational
- Clear path to exits visible
- Light fixtures regularly cleaned and maintained

Poor lighting leads to mistakes and accidents. Test your lighting by ensuring you can read fine print comfortably at your workbenches and tool stations.

Ventilation and Dust Control

Maintain clean air through:

- Dust collection system operational
- Air filtration system running
- Windows accessible for fresh air
- Respirators clean and readily available
- Floor swept regularly
- Dust-producing tools connected to collection

Remember that the finest dust particles pose the greatest health risk because they remain airborne longest and penetrate deepest into your lungs.

Tool Safety

Each tool requires specific safety considerations:

Power Tool Safety

Before using any power tool:

- Guards in place and functioning
- Power cords inspected for damage
- Tool unplugged during blade changes
- Work area clear of obstacles
- Push sticks and blocks available

- Emergency stop accessible
- Tool rest gaps minimal
- Blade/bit sharp and appropriate for task

Develop the habit of unplugging power tools when making adjustments - this simple step prevents many serious accidents.

Hand Tool Safety

Maintain hand tool safety through:
- Tools sharp and well-maintained
- Handles secure and undamaged
- Tools stored properly when not in use
- Cutting tools covered when stored
- Work surface stable
- Proper technique used
- First aid kit nearby

Sharp tools are actually safer than dull ones because they require less force to use, giving you better control.

Emergency Preparedness

Being ready for emergencies can mean the difference between a minor incident and a serious one:

First Aid Preparation

Maintain and regularly check:

- First aid kit fully stocked
- Emergency numbers posted
- Clear path to exits
- Fire extinguisher charged and accessible
- Eye wash station operational
- Emergency procedure posted
- Basic first aid training current
- Mobile phone accessible

Review emergency procedures regularly - during an emergency is not the time to figure out what to do.

Workshop Operation Checks

Before beginning work each day:

- Fire extinguisher checked
- Emergency exits clear
- First aid supplies verified
- All tools inspected
- Ventilation functioning
- Lighting adequate
- Safety equipment accessible
- Work area organized

Think of this daily check as your pre-flight checklist - it only takes a few minutes but can prevent serious problems.

Troubleshooting Guide

Think of this guide as your workshop detective manual, helping you identify, diagnose, and solve common woodworking problems. Just as a doctor uses symptoms to diagnose an illness, we'll use specific signs to identify and fix woodworking issues.

Cutting Problems and Solutions

Saw Blade Issues

When your cuts aren't coming out as expected, consider these common problems and their solutions:

Blade Burning the Wood
- Symptom: Dark burn marks along cut line
- Diagnosis: Check for these indicators:
    1. Blade speed too slow or fast
    2. Feed rate inappropriate
    3. Blade dull or dirty
    4. Wood pinching blade

Solution Approach:
1. Clean blade thoroughly using blade cleaner
2. Check blade sharpness with the reflection test
3. Adjust feed rate - should feel smooth, not forced
4. Ensure proper blade tension

5. Use appropriate blade for material

Rough or Splintered Cuts
- Symptom: Ragged edges or tear-out
- Potential Causes:
 1. Wrong blade for material
 2. Incorrect tooth count
 3. Poor backing support
 4. Improper feed direction

Resolution Steps:
1. Match blade tooth count to material thickness
2. Use zero-clearance insert
3. Support work piece properly
4. Score cut line on cross-grain cuts

Joinery Problems

Joint Fit Issues

When joints aren't coming together properly:

Loose Joints
- Symptoms:
 1. Visible gaps
 2. Joint rocks or moves
 3. Glue doesn't hold

Diagnostic Process:
1. Check measuring tools for accuracy
2. Verify setup hasn't shifted
3. Examine cutting tools for wear
4. Test on scrap material

Solution Implementation:
1. Reset and calibrate tools
2. Use setup blocks for consistency
3. Make test cuts before final pieces
4. Consider joint reinforcement options

Tight Joints
- Symptoms:
 1. Parts won't fully seat
 2. Joint requires excessive force
 3. Wood splitting when assembled

Correction Approach:
1. Make minor adjustments (0.005" at a time)
2. Test fit frequently
3. Check for debris in joint
4. Verify wood moisture content

Finishing Problems

Surface Finish Issues

Common finishing problems often have straightforward solutions:

Blotchy Finish
- Symptoms:
  1. Uneven color absorption
  2. Dark and light patches
  3. Irregular sheen

Diagnosis Steps:
1. Test wood porosity
2. Check wood preparation
3. Examine application technique
4. Verify product compatibility

Solution Process:
1. Apply wood conditioner
2. Sand progressively through grits
3. Use consistent application technique
4. Allow proper drying time between coats

Bubbles in Finish
- Symptoms:
  1. Surface not smooth

2. Visible air bubbles

3. Rough texture

Resolution Approach:

1. Adjust application temperature

2. Thin finish if necessary

3. Use proper application tools

4. Allow finish to settle before use

Wood Movement Problems

Warping and Twisting

When wood doesn't stay flat:

Cupping
- Symptoms:
  1. Board edges higher or lower than center
  2. Panel shape like a shallow bowl
  3. Movement increases over time

Prevention and Correction:

1. Store wood properly before use

2. Allow for proper acclimation

3. Use proper panel construction techniques

4. Consider wood grain orientation

Twisting

- Symptoms:
  1. Board corners not in same plane
  2. Progressive worsening
  3. Assembly difficulties

Solution Steps:
1. Check wood moisture content
2. Verify proper storage conditions
3. Use appropriate construction methods
4. Consider alternative wood species

Tool Maintenance Issues

Tool Performance Problems

When tools aren't performing as expected:

Planer Snipe
- Symptoms:
  1. Deeper cut at board ends
  2. Inconsistent thickness
  3. Visible dips at endpoints

Correction Process:
1. Adjust infeed/outfeed tables
2. Support long boards properly
3. Reduce cutting depth

4. Maintain consistent feed pressure

Router Tear-out
- Symptoms:
  1. Splintered edges
  2. Rough surface
  3. Grain pulling

Solution Implementation:
1. Adjust feed direction
2. Change bit speed
3. Take multiple shallow passes
4. Use appropriate bit for material

Resource Directory

Let me help you navigate through the vast world of woodworking resources, organizing them in a way that makes sense for both beginners and experienced craftspeople. Think of this directory as your roadmap to woodworking knowledge, connecting you with the tools, information, and community you need to grow in your craft.

Educational Resources

Online Learning Platforms

The digital age has transformed how we learn woodworking. These platforms offer structured learning experiences:

Wood Whisperer Guild (www.thewoodwhisperer.com)
- In-depth project tutorials
- Technique demonstrations
- Members-only content
- Active community forums
- Focus on fine furniture making

Fine Woodworking Online (www.finewoodworking.com)
- Comprehensive video library
- Detailed project plans
- Expert techniques
- Tool reviews
- Printable resources

Popular Woodworking (www.popularwoodworking.com)
- Project plans ranging from beginner to advanced
- Historical woodworking techniques
- Tool reviews and comparisons
- Digital magazine archive
- Video tutorials

YouTube Channels Worth Following

These channels offer free, high-quality woodworking content:

Matt Estlea
- Focus on hand tool techniques
- Detailed process breakdowns
- Beginner-friendly explanations
- Traditional joinery methods

Paul Sellers
- Traditional woodworking methods
- Hand tool expertise
- Project-based learning
- Fundamental skills development

Rob Cosman
- Advanced joinery techniques
- Tool selection guidance
- Sharpening tutorials

- Professional tips and tricks

Material Resources

Lumber Suppliers

Understanding where to source quality materials is crucial:

Online Retailers:
- Bell Forest Products: Exotic and domestic hardwoods
- Cook Woods: Specialty burls and figured wood
- Woodworkers Source: Wide variety of species
- Highland Hardwoods: Custom millwork services

Tips for Local Sourcing:
- Build relationships with local sawmills
- Join woodworking clubs for supplier recommendations
- Check architectural salvage yards
- Network with other woodworkers

Tool Suppliers

Quality tools are essential for quality work:

High-End Tools:
- Lie-Nielsen Toolworks: Premium hand tools
- Veritas (Lee Valley): Innovative woodworking tools
- Bridge City Tool Works: Precision instruments

- Festool: Professional power tools

Mid-Range Options:
- Wood River: Quality hand planes
- DeWalt: Reliable power tools
- Narex: Affordable chisels
- Grizzly: Shop machinery

Professional Development

Woodworking Schools

For hands-on learning experiences:

North Bennett Street School (Boston, MA)
- Traditional craftsmanship
- Full-time programs
- Workshop series
- Professional certification

The Krenov School (Fort Bragg, CA)
- Fine furniture making
- Nine-month programs
- Summer workshops
- Advanced techniques

Professional Organizations

Join these groups for networking and growth:

The Furniture Society
- Professional development
- Annual conferences
- Member exhibitions
- Networking opportunities

American Association of Woodturners
- Local chapters
- Educational resources
- Insurance programs
- Technical support

Community Resources

Online Forums

Connect with other woodworkers:

Lumberjocks.com
- Project sharing
- Technical discussions
- Tool reviews
- Community support

Wood Talk Forum
- Active discussion boards
- Expert advice
- Project feedback
- Tool recommendations

Local Resources

Find support in your community:

Woodworking Clubs
- How to find local clubs
- Benefits of membership
- Meeting schedules
- Group purchases

Community Workshops
- Shared tool access
- Learning opportunities
- Project space
- Expert guidance

Technical Resources

Software and Planning Tools

Digital tools to enhance your woodworking:

SketchUp
- 3D design software
- Project planning
- Plugin availability
- Free web version

CutList Optimizer
- Material optimization
- Cutting diagrams
- Waste reduction
- Cost calculation

Reference Materials

Essential information at your fingertips:

Wood Database (wood-database.com)
- Species information
- Working properties
- Pricing guidance
- Sustainability data

Forest Products Laboratory
- Technical data
- Research papers
- Wood properties
- Industry standards

Glossary

Let me guide you through the essential terminology used in woodworking, explaining not just what each term means, but how it relates to your work in the shop. Think of this glossary as your translator for the language of woodworking, helping you understand both historical terms and modern usage.

A

Adze
A traditional tool with a curved blade set perpendicular to the handle, used for rough shaping of wood. Imagine a horizontal axe used to hollow out bowls or roughly shape timber. The tool dates back thousands of years and remains useful for certain sculptural work today.

Annual Rings
These are the growth layers of a tree, visible as concentric circles in the end grain. Understanding annual rings helps you predict wood movement and select grain patterns. Each ring represents one year of growth, with early wood (lighter) and late wood (darker) forming the distinctive pattern.

Arbor

The main shaft of a power tool that holds the cutting blade or bit. You'll encounter this term most often when selecting saw blades or changing cutters, as the arbor size must match your tool precisely.

B

Baluster

A vertical support member, commonly seen in railings and staircases. These elements combine both structural and decorative functions, requiring careful attention to both strength and appearance in their creation.

Bevel

An angled cut or surface that isn't 90 degrees. Understanding bevels is crucial for both joinery and decorative work. The term can refer to both the cut itself and the tool used to mark or create it.

Bird's Eye

A distinctive figure pattern in wood, appearing as small, round patterns resembling birds' eyes. Most commonly found in maple, this highly prized figure results from natural growth conditions that aren't fully understood.

C

Chamfer

Similar to a bevel but typically referring to a 45-degree angle cut removing a square edge. Chamfers serve both decorative and practical purposes, such as softening edges and preventing splintering.

Checking

The splitting of wood along the grain as it dries, distinct from normal seasonal movement. Understanding checking helps you identify problematic wood before using it in your projects.

Counterbore

A flat-bottomed hole drilled to allow a screw head to sit below the surface. This differs from countersinking in that it creates a cylindrical rather than conical depression.

D

Dado

A channel cut across the grain of a board, used commonly in casework and shelving. Understanding dados is essential for furniture construction, as they provide both alignment and mechanical strength to joints.

Dovetail

A strong woodworking joint resembling a dove's spread tail, used for centuries in fine furniture making. The interlocking angles create mechanical strength while showcasing the craftsperson's skill.

G

Grain

The direction and pattern of wood fiber growth. Understanding grain direction affects everything from cutting technique to structural strength and finishing results. Think of grain as the wood's muscle fibers, determining how it will behave when worked.

M

Mortise and Tenon

A fundamental woodworking joint where a projecting tenon fits into a matching mortise (hole). This ancient joint remains one of the strongest ways to join wood, especially for frame construction.

P

Plumb
Perfectly vertical, as indicated by a plumb bob or level. Essential for construction and installation work, plumb relates to gravity rather than any existing structure.

Q

Quarter Sawn
Lumber cut so the annual rings run roughly perpendicular to the face of the board. This cutting method produces more stable lumber and often reveals distinctive ray fleck patterns, especially in oak.

S

Spalting
A coloration pattern in wood caused by fungal growth, often creating striking black lines and patterns. While potentially beautiful, spalted wood requires careful assessment as excessive spalting can weaken the wood.

T

Through Tenon

A mortise and tenon joint where the tenon passes completely through the mortised piece and is visible on the other side. Often used both for strength and decorative effect.

Would you like me to elaborate on any of these terms or explain additional woodworking terminology?

Made in the USA
Las Vegas, NV
01 May 2025

21571960R00203